Blogging Florida

Snowbirds on the Run

by Marla J. Selvidge

Blogging Florida

A Snowbird on the Run

Marla J. Selvidge

Roseville Publications

ISBN-978-0-9967658-1-7

Many thanks to my dear friends

Mary Kaye Golden,

Evelyn "Lois" Gray,

and Ginny McTighe

who kept me sane during the long,

and lonely months of Covid 19.

And, to

Thomas Charles Hemling,

who made the adventure possible!

Table of Contents

All photographs by Marla J. Selvidge and Thomas C. Hemling except where noted. Permissions are underneath photos and illustrations.

Prelude to a New Life!

How does anyone decide that they are going to leave their happy home and move to Florida? Camping and RVing for more than thirty years, we decided to try to find a snowbird palace in the south. Oil land (Texas) and the fumes did not appeal to us.

For decades we had spent at least one week a year exploring Florida coasts and cruises. One year we landed a two-week stay at Sebastian Inlet State Park. Gorgeous is an understatement. There was the inlet, the pelicans, the fisher people and the enticing beautiful white beach. Water surrounds you. Convinced that Florida was a place to spend a few months in the winter, we began looking for places to park our Class A Motorhome. How hard could it be?

It was beyond wild! Many of the RV resorts catered to families who had been renting for lifetimes. There was no room at the Inn. Other parks were so small that we could not even turn the 40-foot Class A. Many RV resorts were in decline. Others were high ends costing between $125 and $150 a night with no guarantee that they would have an open reservation. We checked out about twenty different RV resorts from Palm Beach to Orlando and found nothing that would work for us.

We did not want to camp on sand or rock. Our rig was too large. (In one RV resort our coach sank down in the sand and had to be towed.) Several resorts were specialized and only allowed (for instance) Air Streams. Some did not allow pets. The restrictions did not matter because everything was booked up for years.

Finally, we heard about The Great Outdoors RV Resort. On our way home we stopped to assess the community. The problem was that no one would allow us to view the community. No real estate agents were available, and the rules prohibited us from driving around the gated community. Finally, someone took pity on us and gave us a two-hour pass. (If we had been locals, we could have just told them that we were going to dine at the Blue Heron or golf. But we were clueless.)

We drove around on the main drag, Plantation, but it did not help us to decide whether we could stay a few weeks or a few days in the winter. No one had any information for us. We headed home.

Another Year of Searching

After landing another reservation at Sebastian Inlet State Park we discovered that The Great Outdoors (TGO) rented spots for $70 a night. With an MLS Real Estate agent in hand, the search was launched. But the MLS agent would/could not show us TGO listed properties. She told us that they would pay her virtually nothing for a sale. TGO Real Estate agents do not belong to MLS.

Eventually, months later, we found a TGO Real Estate agent that would answer the phone. But she wasn't exactly forthcoming with information about renting. TGO Real Estate agents hid from us the fact that others at TGO who owned property rented it out for months at a time, and that there were For Sale by Owner properties for sale. The TGO Real Estate Agents were not about to help us find something that was offered by an owner. So, we were driven toward buying instead of renting. It is part of the TGO plan for the future. Our ignorance was their win.

Most of the time we did not really understand what we were touring. What was the difference? How do you know market value? How do you compare the Executive Suites? (We call them "huts.") The agent provided no information to help us understand anything. It was a mission of looking and seeing. Can you really believe this?

To be fair, the husband of our agent had a heart attack and she had to leave the search. We were handed over into the hands of the seller's agent and he really did his job. He took care of the seller.

All of the driveways and Executive Suites that we toured were in need of major renovations. Furnishings were at least 20 or more years old. Apparently, people who vacation in Florida, don't want to spend their time on upkeep. There is also the age factor. As people live into their eighties and nineties, they don't have the strength, determination, or finances to remake their vacation or permanent homes.

Finally, we made a bid on a port with a small executive suite. An executive suite is a small house. A port is a large metal garage with an open area. The owners sent back an agreement which read, "AS IS." We went back to view the property again and found significant wood rot and that the port was unstable. To fix the port alone would cost twenty to thirty thousand dollars. Nix that one!

In the end we purchased an 1100 square foot executive suite on a very long driveway. Problems surfaced. The inspector did not do his job. There were leaks in the roof and more. He had to return his inspection fee to us. Throughout the entire process of buying this property we felt as if TGO Real Estate was controlling us. We discovered so many problems and they knew just the right guy to handle it. Right!

On the day we were to sign a contract, neither I nor my spouse were convinced that we should do it. So, we flipped a coin and bought the property. And we have spent the last three and half years renovating it. Some days we wish we had lost that coin.

Tradition in some communities in Florida is to sell a property with its furnishings. This may sound like a windfall, but it is more like a breaking-back story. The furnishings in the hut we purchased were greasy and filthy. And they covered almost every inch of the hut. New Paint had not touched the walls in years, and no one seemed to bother to clean the windows (or anything else) that were encased with dead bugs.

When we inspected the property, it was very dark inside. The colors were mostly browns, and the windows were covered. When we tore down the window coverings after we bought the suite, the filth emerged. We filled a huge SPCA truck with all the furniture and dated "crap." Our seller's Real Estate Agent said that we could sell the stuff, he kept looking at things and wanted them. Does this ever happen to you? We will come to these issues again later!

While millions of tourists are desperately trying to find a place to rent for the winter in Florida. Our hut works well for us. We don't need reservations.

The remainder of this book catalogs excerpts from my blog, "Motoring with Marla," www.motoringwithmarla.com. You and I are going to explore Florida together from the point of view of a snowbird. Happy flying!

MYFLORIDA.COM
DECAL
SAMPLE
SUNSHINE STATE

Chapter One

Two Drifters Off to See the World

"There's such a lovely world to see...."

We know the route well, across Arkansas. But how did we miss the town of "Toad Suck?" Yes, and in an online poll it won the honor of being the "worst" named town in the USA. There is even a Toad Suck Campground and motorcycle dealer! It is no joke!

Crossing Arkansas on highway 40 is more than dangerous with twelve eighteen wheelers to one car tooling down the road. Some of the trucks were in caravans as far as you could see.

Our goal for the day was to land at the birthplace (so-called) of Elvis Presley. We have visited this holy site a couple of times but had missed exploring the rejuvenated town of Tupelo, Mississippi.

Tupelo will welcome you. Tupelo Hardware Store where Elvis' mom bought his first guitar, was beyond charming. Bolts, etc., were stored in old wooden boxes. A well-coiffed and dressed public relations lady guarding the door, was full of stories and love for Elvis. "People just don't understand what a wonderful man he was. He influenced so many people and came from nothing." (Pic below is from the hardware store.)

After our stroll through town, we stopped at a bakery, of course! They were also selling chances to win a 6-caliber pistol. Is that legal?

Elvis was not at home when we arrived. We circled the home built (supposedly) by his father. More statues had been added to the landscape since our last pilgrimage, and there was more "stuff" to do and view while worshipping his little homeplace. Even a busload of international tourists, carrying hefty box-lunches, loved the museum and their moment of silence with Elvis.

Elvis enveloped my life for a while. On a long-ago trip to Oklahoma, we heard Elvis sing, "I have never been to heaven, but I have been to Oklahoma," as we crossed into Oklahoma from Kansas. (How does this happen?) Elvis had never been on my favorites list. I had picked up a couple of Elvis CDs to listen in our RV because they were so cheap.

It was odd. I thought he sounded like my Tennessee-born father who passed when I was in my twenties. So, I decided to research his life and music. A couple of years later I ended up teaching a college course entitled "Elvis. Memphis Messiah," and writing his life story in, "For the Love of Elvis."

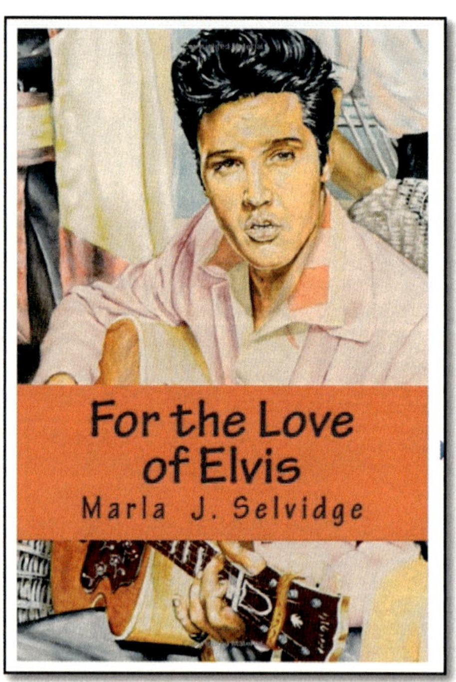

Heading toward Birmingham, the state sign, "Sweet Home Alabama" welcomed us! Remember that tune? We stayed overnight at the very tired Queen Peach RV Resort.

Sweet home Alabama
Where the skies are so blue
Sweet home Alabama
Lord, I'm coming home to you, here I come

Savannah, new territory for us, was our final stop on this leg of the journey before we hit Florida. Crossing the Moon River (Yes, the Moon River), we entered an off-world experience at Skidaway Island State Park. Batman would have loved trolling around here. Spanish Moss reaches out and almost suffocates you. Don't touch it because it harbors chiggers!

The whole park felt like a cave. Kudzu (that vicious killing vine from Japan), Red Cedars, Palm Trees, Oaks, and Maples created a surreal and gruesome landscape. In the evenings, you could not see two feet in front of you. During the day the sun never flickered through the gnarled mess. Save me quick, Wonder Woman!

A fella camper extolled the beauty of the medieval forest to us. I told her that I felt claustrophobic. Her husband asked us if we were from "out west." (Is Kansas City out west?) They said they hear the claustrophobic thing a lot from people who live in Colorado and big sky country! This is "cocoon country," and they loved it!

People rave about Savannah. It was not what we expected. Certainly, it had plenty of graceful historic buildings, but I had a great need to take a pressure hose with bleach and wash everything clean. Talking with a bartender, we both agreed that Savannah was a lot like New Orleans. To me, it was an outdoor museum that needed a bit of upgrading and TLC. While walking around the historic district, we did not talk to single person who had a southern accent. We heard plenty of other languages. Even the store owners did not speak with a southern accent. Is Savannah really Southern? After leaving Savannah, we headed for Florida, and are now residing in sparkling Sebastian Inlet State Park where the temperatures are in the seventies. Join us!

Chapter Two

The Borg Invaded Sebastian Inlet

The Borg have invaded Sebastian Inlet. Sebastian Inlet Park is a Park like no other. Beauty beckons for you to return to Sebastian Inlet State Park in Florida. It is located where the 121-mile Indian River flows into the Atlantic Ocean. Any time of night or day you can see water flowing in and out of the Inlet. Sometimes flocks of white Pelicans take rides on water that whisks them out to the Atlantic. My daily 90-minute walk included talking to hundreds of different birds, fish, and people fishing up a storm. Water circles the campground! Can anything get any better?

During our first morning beach walk, we found people fishing who were not well-clothed and spoke languages that we did not recognize. They were immigrants, but from where? I wondered if they lived on the beach? or the jungle nearby!

Everywhere you look at Sebastian Inlet someone is fishing. Heads and faces are bundled like women wearing the hijab. (Are they hiding their identity?) As they walk or bike, dragging behind them are small trailers filled with paraphernalia. They fish off the rocks, the docks, boats, the bridge walkway, on the beach, from bicycles, and even from their cars.

This morning I saw a man cooking fish for breakfast on a little gas burner sitting on the back gate of his very old pickup truck. He was not camping. He was homeless because I saw the inside of his truck with his mattresses and belongings. If he was camping, he would have been at a regular site!

On my way back to our campsite, I passed by four male campers in a row standing at their respective picnic tables facing in the same direction, fiddling with their fishing gear. It could have been a scene from a movie!

Kayaking and More

Kayaking is grand on the Indian river. Tom has experienced Dolphins swimming around him and paddled right over a shark. Yesterday, a huge fish jumped across his kayak. Park rangers have warned that there are alligators and harmful jellyfish just waiting to snap at a tourist. But the kayakers don't mind. Adventure is the goal of the day.

The Borg

During our first week at Sebastian, we spied the steel dredging contraptions out in the water, but they were broken. They did not make a sound. A cyclops of a light watched us. Then suddenly there was a loud hum, and something that sounded like thunder started the gigantic beating heart. The steel contraptions came alive and began bringing sand through three-foot around rubber hoses to somewhere south of the Inlet.

Throughout the night the heartbeat continued and rattled our motorhome. We did not bargain for this invasion of the Borg.

If you have watched Star Trek over the years, you know about the aliens, the Borg. They are "cybernetic organisms, linked in a hive mind called the Collective." They are to be feared. I felt like these cybernetic organisms, the dredging machines, were killing the Inlet, or at least taking over its mind. (You know the Hindus believe rivers are divine!) When I spoke with a volunteer at the park and told him about my idea that the Borg had taken over, he said, "I think you are correct."

Sunsets on cruise ships are surreal experiences. But, here, at Sebastian they are even more mind-melting. This evening as we walked the Indian River, watching the sun disappear, we smelled oil. *Yes, the Borg had killed the Inlet.* They have poisoned it with diesel. We could see the oil pooling around the edge of the Inlet. Where are the reporters? (This might be a bit dramatic!)

Crews of men, dressed in yellow vests, swarmed the Inlet while we slept. Poof! The oil was gone!

Finding a Winter Home for our RV

We began visiting resorts to find a place that we might rent, as you read in the introduction. None of the resorts met our high expectations. Like Texas, Florida resorts jam RVs together. There is no room to breathe. They choke your vision and your lungs.

Sebastian Inlet is a wonderful place to camp for only $26 a day. (If you are a Florida resident, the cost is only $13.00 a day.) We have no one camping in front or the back of us and there are at least 20-30 feet between camp sites with open space. The site next to us is so large that you could put six RVs in it. But you can only camp here for two weeks at a time not three months.

We began our search again this year. (This is a repeat.) With an MLS realtor at TGO, we visited RV pad sites with executive suites or as I call them "huts!" They are no bigger than 10X10 feet and usually house a washer/dryer, makeshift kitchen, and shower. Many of the units we previewed were filled with mold and mildew.

We also visited resorts where you could rent or purchase a pad. (A pad is a cement driveway with all the utilities you need to hook up your RV.) The problem we faced was "junk" and flags and barking dogs. We don't want to spend a winter camping near someone who has 30 years of precious possessions sitting out in front of their RV. (They are like the homesteaders we met in Alaska.) We like areas to be neat and clean with a little elbow room and a view.

Chapter Three

Space Coast Xmas under the Palm Trees

Usually, Tom and I try to escape Xmas by leaving the country. The shopping and frantic rush to make purchases that leads to gridlock in the stores and on the highways is too much for us. One year, to our dismay when visiting India, we were greeted with Xmas music and large decorated Xmas trees at our first hotel. Escape to Morocco. Very few are singing Jingle Bells in that country.

TGO has Changed Our Minds.

It is like they have *Christmas fever*. So, as you have read, we purchased a hut at The Great Outdoors and have become Florida residents. This was our first Xmas at TGO.

TGO residents regress back to childhood and celebrate XMAS for weeks. Wreaths are attached to the back of their golf carts. Christmas lights blink and Xmas music can be heard for blocks. Even the trucks who service TGO residents are decorated.

At least two streets have Xmas displays that light up the skies at night. During the day, you can tour the street with blow-up Xmas figures. I especially like the one where Santa is piloting a rocket. Every yard, the whole street, is lit up at night! Wonder if aliens can see it? WOW! And on the main drag, called Plantation, there are pink Flamingo's pulling Santa's sleigh!

At TGO, they serve free cookies and drinks at the local church and have created an evening where decorated houses are open to the public. On one Friday, scores of decorated golf carts parade through the compound. Early in the fall, the Nature Center had a sale of Xmas items. Little did we know that these items would be on display just about everywhere.

The Volkswagen Christmas Wagon below was a late arrival to the parade because the sides fell off when they surged toward the street. Quick thinking got it back together.

Tom, my partner and spouse, joined the parade. Notice the lights on his handlebars. He was the only one peddling! Every condo-area throughout the park has its own decorated Xmas sign--with lights. You can't miss them!

Underneath TGO Xmas trees (Palm trees) are all sorts of creatures including alligators and armadillos. This morning I was overrun by guys in their 80's circling streets in their very red and very expensive motorcycles. Other guys in their 80's were also driving decorated BMW and Audi convertibles. Huh!

Shopping at Be(a)lls (my favorite department store) the other day, we spotted a palm tree with Xmas lights that was half price. But it was still too pricey for us. After Xmas, I am going back to see if it is still for sale. Who me? Yes you! Below is one of the cutest Xmas scenes!

(The guys below are living it up!)

Apollo Beach (What a name!)

On one afternoon close to Santa day, we visited Apollo Beach on the Canaveral National Sea Shore. Right in front of the Visitor's Center was a rocket-ship sleigh waiting for Santa to Arrive.

This sleigh was the most unusual that I have ever seen in my life. Wonder if someone from TGO helped to design it?

This chapter won't describe our experience watching a rocket launch, (that will come later) but I did want to draw attention to the fact that SpaceX sends objects out into space about the same time that Santa arrives. *Watch out Santa!*

Chapter Four

Living the Myth at Cape Canaveral

As a child, I would lay in the grass watching for Sputnik to cross the horizon. I wanted to know who was in that shiny little dot in the sky. I also remember watching astronauts walk on the moon, and then, trying to explain it to locals in Sierra Leone. They did not believe me!

I admit it. I am a recovering Trekkie! Glued to the TV, I watched many of the Star Trek franchises and read extensively in Science Fiction when I was younger. Do you remember: James T. Kirk (a role model), Jean-Luc Picard, Kathryn Janeway, and one of my favorites, Benjamin Sisko? Now we are living that space and star dream in Florida in the shadow of the Kennedy Space Center/Cape Canaveral.

We are not alone! The myth of space penetrates businesses everywhere along the Space Coast. Here is a short list of some of the astral names people use:

Costal Dental, Astrotech Space, **Rocket City Real Estate**, Space Shirts, **Space Museum**, Solar Lube, **Rocket Car Wash**, Space Coast Credit Union, **Space Coast Pawn**, Warbird Museum, **Space Coast Ice Cream**-- and so many more!

Titusville (Our Town)

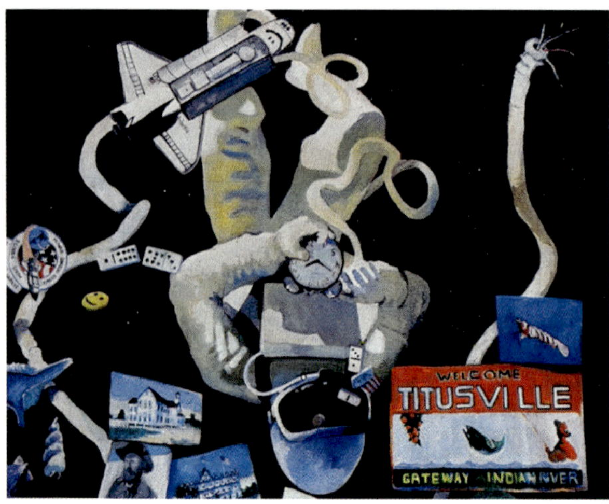

Titusville even offers a map showing approved designated viewing areas of launches. Last spring, we were standing in our neighbor's driveway (at night) when we heard this tremendous sound and then shaking below us. We looked East and saw a ball of fire take off from Canaveral. It seemed as if it was a scene from "Dr. Strangelove," and the atom bomb had just exploded. We had no idea that launches could be so powerful and visually compelling. Notice all the specs in the sky below. Those were planes. Airplanes start buzzing the area before and during a launch and fly on either side of a rocket.

Our friends, *Igor and the Red Elvises*, perform regularly in clubs around the Space Center. The fans love his rocket tunes. Here is one for you! "I am a Rocket Man."

"Looking at Earth through telescope
My spaceship is clean, and I love my job
Music of space crawls in my ear;
I'm dreaming of girls and six-pack of beer

I AM A ROCKET MAN!
I AM A ROCKET MAN!"

Launches and the Fans

Crowds were gathering at the edge of Indian River, right across from Cape Canaveral. People were parked on the grass with lawn chairs by their sides. There was an air of excitement. *We were all smiling!*

As we anticipated the launch, I was struck by how orderly, polite, and diverse the crowd was. Finally, we saw a flash of light as SpaceX launched a Falcon 9 rocket headed for the Space Station. The rocket seemed so small compared with others we have seen while staying in Melbourne years ago.

As it sped toward the Space Station the sound was deafening. Billowing dark clouds of exhaust from the rocket at Cape Canaveral reflected millions of flying birds who had been shocked or displaced by the rocket launch. What a sight!

All of us were looking up. No one moved. Within a couple of minutes, we lost sight of the rocket. But people were still looking up. I think we wanted another rocket to launch or maybe we were just worshipping the technology that sent that piece of steel into space.

Maybe we wanted to be in that rocket? Some left the river right after the launch, but others stayed and kept staring at the sky as we departed the restaurant, Dogs R Us.

It was a sacred moment.

Is it a Bird, Is it a Plane, No, its ...

I have (fortunately) lived through all of the space adventures so far. There was Sputnik, the monkey astronauts, the men on the moon, abductions, landed aliens, the space accidents, the space station, and more. But could I name all of the astronauts and missions? My grade would be an "F." Brevard Museum of History and Natural Science makes a point of informing us that the first woman astronaut/cosmonaut was from the USSR, Valentina Tereshkova. Did you know that? I did not! Below is a *real* suit that an astronaut wore into space!

Titusville has many mind-boggling space exhibits. Now the U.S.A. is launching a Space Force (maybe?), and it will be just across the river from us! Names of the historic astronauts are everywhere. Here is one etched into a sidewalk.

Just like the movie stars out west, and the music notes on the sidewalk in Memphis, each astronaut has their name embedded in concrete. I think space adventure of the 20th century was different. We were exploring space, going where no one has gone before. Now the launches are more like a business and the competitive future of controlling space around the earth. We are still in awe of the rockets and astronauts, but people are not clamoring to install their names on a walk of fame. Below is one of my favorite photos!

The image captures how I felt walking through all of the displays. I was just floating in space. Next time you visit the Kennedy Space Center, stop, and have lunch in Titusville and visit all the space displays!

Chapter Five

Titusville. Living it up in Space City.

The Coronavirus was coming our way! They shut down the tours at the Refuge and at the Brevard Museum of History and Natural Science. I voluntarily left the Visitor's Desk at the Merritt Island National Refuge. Eventually it was closed and opened again on weekends.

There are at least 100 restaurants in Titusville. Loyd Have Mercy was recently featured on the Food Channel. Many of the mom-and-pop family restaurants post their daily offerings on a white board. The paper menu that is handed to you is just a suggestion, freshly cooked food is on the Board.

One of our favorite diners is Good Thymes where the owner personally comes to your table and greets you. Her personality is bigger than life. Another hotspot is Steve's Diner that is owned by John.

Recently we discovered Pier 220 right on the intra-costal highway. The setting is beyond gorgeous. Outside you can dine right above the water, at the bar, or on a sandy beach while listening to live music. Inside it is calmer with a great view of the Indian River and boats coming and going. After a meal you can walk the pier and talk to people who are shrimping. This is as good of an experience as one on the island of St. Croix or maybe better!

Shrimpers use lights to attract the catch. What a beautiful site right under the Max Brewer Bridge to the Merritt Island National Refuge.

Titusville and Mims

In March we were invited to a **Black History Celebration** at Eastern Florida State College. Our new friend, Lois (center) invited us. Her daughter Tara was on the planning committee of the event.

The evening explored the life of Harry and Harriette Moore, civil rights activists in the 20th century. In 1951, they were responsible for more than 100,000 African Americans signing up to vote. For this hard work, their home was bombed and both of them were murdered. Of course, the perpetrators were never found.

They were not the only persons of color to be murdered in Florida. Florida has a horrendous history of stealing the land and the lives from peoples of color who called Florida home. Read about their lives and the Black Seminoles, if you ever get a chance!

Located in Mims, a memorial park has been created in their name. It serves as an educational center. Below is a replica of their beautiful home.

Shell Mounds of Florida (Just East of Titusville)

Since volunteering as a docent at the Brevard Museum of History and Natural Science, I have become very interested in the shell mounds that are found along the Eastern Coast of the United States. Canaveral National Seashore has many mounds and features "Turtle Mound" that rises 50 feet above the water. Originally thought to be middens or garbage dumps, scholars now think that they were foundations of ancient villages. And these mounds are found along oceans and rivers all over the world. Below is an artist's conception of mounds.

This illustration of numerous shell mounds at the Turner River Shellworks site in Ten Thousand Islands, Florida, is based on archaeological evidence. Credit: MARTIN PATE, COURTESY MARGO SCHWADRON, NPS

We visited Turtle Mound, Seminole Rest, and on another day, hiked Hontoon State Island Park to discover a shell mound. No one really understands these mounds. I hope to do more research and present a lecture on the topic for the National Park Service in the future, after Covid.

Below is a diagram of shell mounds found along the Canaveral Coast. When we visited Turtle Mound it was closed for repairs. So, we hiked around it because the walkway was closed. Standing 50 feet tall, it may have seemed like a skyscraper to the indigenous residents. Near Turtle Mound is Seminole Rest.

There are several shell mounds around and under the preserved 19th century buildings at Seminole Rest. Those mounds date back to 2,000 B.C.E. The Park Service, through kiosks, takes you through the history of the site. Owners of the houses, such as Wesley H. Snyder, would not sell their property because they wanted to protect and preserve the shell mounds. You can walk all around the homes and down to a boardwalk on the Indian River. They are preserving the mounds by directing traffic to stay on a constructed boardwalk. This place is now well-preserved and a treat to visit.

Hontoon Island State Park

How do you recognize shell mounds? Since living in Florida, I have walked on a lot of properties that had visible seashells on pathways. Most notably, I have seen them on golf courses. I don't know if the properties were built on shell mounds, or they dug into other mounds and used the shells for the ground cover.

Over the years, shell mounds have been used for fertilizer, foundations of homes, and to build roads/paths. The shells are strong and stick together to make a sturdy site for anything. The problem is that when you dig into the mounds, you destroy history. Can you see the shells below?

Hontoon is a great place to visit. Located only a few miles Northeast of Titusville, it is an easy day trip. In order to hike the island, a pontoon boat gives you a free ride. Only six people are allowed on the boat at time. It feels as if you have a chauffeur.

The island sports a very good museum about the mounds and several hiking trails that take you to the mounds. We were hoping to see a huge white mound. When we arrived at the end of the trail, we found that the mound had been built on a riverbank above the St. Johns River. We were actually standing on part of it. The best way to view the mound would be by boat.

Below is a photo from the Hontoon Museum. Look closely at the reconstructed slice of a shell mound on the left. The reason that there is dark dirt on top is that the indigenous peoples have been gone for more than 500 years. Leaves and trees fell on top of the mounds and created the mixture of shells and dirt.

Chapter Six

Covid-19 Shut Down Blues

"When we close our minds, it is as if we voluntarily imprison ourselves in a tight and narrow world."

White Sands Website

Locked in place, how do you cope? We needed a release from the anxiety we were feeling. Tom and I decided that we were going to pretend that we were in another country. As tourists and explorers, we tooled around the outskirts of the great Disney Kingdom and the Space Coast. We decided that we were not going to talk to anyone because, at that time, it was too dangerous. And it still is in 2022.

Anyone can do this, even with the lockdown as a distant memory. Explore your community. Google religions, temples, mosques, synagogues, and more. Discover the wonderful religions and peoples who live near you.

White Sands Buddhist Center

One of Tom's new friends told us about White Sands Buddhist Center in Mims. We were skeptical that something so wonderful could be found so close, in Mims. Then, we were totally amazed at the serenity and beauty of the place when we found it. The buildings were closed but the grounds were open to the public. We were the only tourists visiting that day.

White Sands includes both Buddhas (images of the living Buddha) and Bodhisattvas (people who give their lives to others). Images can point the way to Nirvana. Nirvana is defined in many ways. The easiest way to explain it is that the person will find the Divine and find release from the pressures of life.

This Reclining Buddha demonstrates how to reach Nirvana by chilling out!

White Sands is sponsored by the Vietnamese government. We have visited many temples in Vietnam, but I did not research what division of Buddhism the Vietnamese followed. White Sands seems to be a mixture of Mahayana and Pure Land Buddhism. Mahayana looks to Bodhisattvas (sort of living Buddhas) to help them reach Nirvana. Pure Land Buddhism, founded in Japan, is modeled after Christianity with a hope for a heavenly life. I think both strains were found on the grounds of White Sands.

Guan Yin (spelled a variety of different ways in different countries) is a bodhisattva who lives to help others. She is one of my favorites because she loves other so much. We found fantastic images of her in Inner Mongolia.

The photo above is a traditional sculpture of the Buddha. He is encouraging people to rest and meditate as a way of overcoming pain and the struggles we face.

White Sands was a welcome relief to the craziness on the news and in the grocery stores. Walking the grounds and viewing the statues put your mind at ease. What a great find!

Religious Structures are Often Hidden

Local governments often write building codes with the express purpose of keeping out faiths unfamiliar to them. Sometimes they put limits on a dome or how a building can be designed or redesigned. This forces religions to create unusual architectures and then, to become even more creative. Sometimes they go underground to create the religious space that meets their needs. Often, they purchase unwanted land, defunct warehouses, or production sites, and build their beautiful buildings inside. From the outside their property looks like it needs repair. From the inside it can be a glorious golden dome of light. White Sands is hidden in a great forest.

Most of the religious properties we visited were not on main streets. The Hindu Temple was built next to an old car dump. Behind a wall of apartments and fences stood the Sikh Temple. And the Jewish Synagogue, from the street, looked like an office building. Of course, no religious structure is safe these days.

The Sikh Temple

South of Orlando. Gurdwara is a place to gather! Nanaksar refers to its division.

Sikhs are generally monotheistic and resist the caste system found within Hinduism in India. The parking lot was empty when we arrived at the temple. Soon, Mr. Singh was greeting us and inviting us for a tour, or at the very least a bite to eat. He was so welcoming. Declining the invitation, we promised we would return.

Manav Mandir Hindu Temple in Melbourne

There were many Hindu temples near Melbourne, perhaps ten, we chose this one.

What a treat! We snuck by the "No Trespassing" sign because the gate was open. *It was like an invitation.* Hindus are often polytheistic. Stories about their gods and goddesses are very entertaining.

Many Indians prefer to call themselves "monotheistic" because they follow the "One, Supreme God" from which all others emanate. Some follow only Shiva or a favorite God or Goddess. One of our favorite Gods is Ganesh(a), bringer of good luck. And what do you know--greeting us on that beautiful day was Ganesh. And we were in luck! The image above is Ganesh. Ganesh is the son of Shiva and Parvati. It is quite a story and too long to rehearse here. Google it if you are interested!

Wat Dhammaram

We also tried to visit an additional Buddhist site south of Orlando that houses monks, but we were not allowed to enter. It was created as a monastery. We will go back after the virus settles down. Exploring other cultures and religions opens your eyes to colorful and creative ways of interpreting life.

Ohev Shalom Jewish Synagogue

I chose this synagogue because of its architecture. We drove right by it because we did not recognize that it was a synagogue. Because of the trees hiding the structure, even after climbing stairs of an adjacent building, I could not take a good photo. The photo below is next to the beautiful front door of the building.

The name Ohev Shalom is a translation of the Hebrew letters in the lamp. "Ohev" means "he loves." And, of course, shalom means "peace."

Holy Land Experience

Have you traveled to Israel? If you have, one of places that most tourists visit is a replica of Jerusalem during the time of Jesus, or the second temple period. It is right behind the Holy Land Hotel. In Orlando, the *Holy Land Experience* complex tries to capture this small replica of Jerusalem on a grand scale. The gates were locked so we were limited on photography. At the front gate stood a handsome soldier who made you feel as if you were entering Roman space. Through this portal you could see the ancient Israelite temple and replicas of other sites in Israel. It is now closed forever.

Explore Your City, Town, Countryside

This is no time to be hunkered down. We met only one person on our religious treks, so we were practicing extreme-social-distancing. Make a plan and visit places that you have never been that are near you. We tried not to stop at public restrooms, so your treks could be about an hour long. We also stopped by a Masjid (mosque) in Titusville, but it was in a small house and not so interesting. What is interesting is that there are Muslims in Titusville.

Today, as we walked along the Indian river, people were holding exercise classes outside. Some were boxing. Many were walking their dogs. There was plenty of space for everyone. So, get out that bicycle, or tricycle, or motorcycle, or .... and explore your world.

This is not the end of our exploring. We have investigated the cities of Mims and Titusville and discovered historic and important sites. In another blog, I will share them with you. So, get out there and enjoy and love your world.

Chapter Seven

Leaving Florida Early was Painful

We drove back to Missouri one month early. It was not what we had planned. But the governor kept making lethal mistakes regarding the virus. A quick check shows almost 30,000 cases and 900 deaths today. (On the day of composing this chapter there were 2,293,980 cases and 36,133 deaths. These numbers will go up.) In the beginning, no one was being tested. To be accurate there are probably thousands of cases that went by the wayside. We have a friend who had the virus and locals would not test her.

Politics and the Health Crisis

The governor of Florida was more concerned with finances than funerals. He allowed students to storm the southern beaches of Florida (Miami-Dade Counties), and this is exactly where the epicenter continues to grow. In a knee-jerk decision he closed the borders from Louisiana and to people traveling from the Northeast. Then, he banned rentals of vacation properties. He forgot that half of the people living on the Florida coast are from the Northeast and have homes in Florida. So TGO (The Great Outdoors RV Resort) had an influx of East Coast people that we had not seen all winter! Shuttered windows on houses opened and the streets filled with people as the virus exploded in New York, New Jersey, and more.

Florida Systems Failed

The governor was pressed to open Florida because the unemployment online system crashed and has only served about 15% of those out of work (at this writing). (Thousands and thousands of people have been furloughed by Disney and other entertainment venues.) Today they reported that one million people had filed for unemployment. The unemployment system was designed to fail because the last governor, Rick Scott, (as I read) wanted to taut his ability to keep people working by making it very difficult to apply for unemployment insurance. It was to be a star on his forehead. Now, the sky is and was falling on the governor and no one can fix the system. We figured that Covid was coming for us soon!

Merritt Island National Refuge

A great highlight in our lives was volunteering at the Refuge. Sadness stalked us as we left. We were both at high risk because of serving so many visiting internationals from the Space Center. I figured that Covid was going to knock on our door, but thankfully, it has not visited us. (Or are we carriers?) With our work schedule gone, we were stuck at TGO for most of the day. Below is a photo taken along Biolab road at the Refuge.

TGO Illusions

TGO is a close-knit community. Socializing is an art. Many think that all they need in life is found at TGO. (Restaurants, golf course, swimming pools, tennis, games, Nature Center, special events, and a scores of clubs.) So, everyone talks to everyone all hours of the day. (hyperbole)

TGO residents protested when the community church cancelled all activities. In spite of the mandatory shutdown, the church kept holding meetings in their parking lot and in people's homes. I argued on Facebook that the virus was airborne, but the ***elect*** paid no attention to the science of the virus. Unforgivably, they pretended that it did not exist. "The blood of Jesus was going to protect them," is a quote I recently heard on TV. This really scared us.

And the virus did come to TGO, again and again and again! Next, there were rumors that the two couples who live on our street had been stranded on a Princess virus ship. They were coming home. They are our neighbors.

Campgrounds were Shut!

We also heard that governors were shutting down public campgrounds and some states were closing private ones. (Our favorite campgrounds were closed.) We were afraid that we would have no place to park during our four-day trek home. We were afraid that we would not make it back to Missouri. We had to leave. It took two days to pack. We left, hoping that we would not be quarantined along the way. One campground threatened to quarantine us 14 days if we stayed with them. (Friends across the street at TGO have a home in Alaska and cannot leave. The border to Canada was closed.)

The Lonely Trek to Cass County

The green grass and Palm trees gave way to an open road with some rest areas closed. And (believe it or not) rest areas on Interstates cannot be found in some states. This is very dangerous for everyone. Trucks end up parking on exits and along the interstate in order to take breaks. Very few automobiles ventured on the interstates we drove. There were trucks in front of us, in back of us, and very close beside us on every highway.

Campground Blues

There were three of these trailers (above) in this campground. I had never seen anything like these anywhere else. They had been resurrected from somewhere. I wondered if they had been in a junk yard and pieced together. In our travels, we see a lot of people living on the edge in campgrounds across the country.

After considerable research, Tom located places for us to park overnight. When we arrived, two or three of the sites had electrical problems. At one place, we had to move twice to find a site where the electrical worked. People stole the breakers out of the units. It is disheartening to see how people live in these less-than-trailer parks.

We called ahead and paid by credit card so that we would not have to meet or talk with anyone. Of course, this did not work all of the time. The places where we stayed were permanent homes for a host of families. We saw very few RV's or motorhomes on the road and only one or two other transients like us in the campgrounds.

I think a lot of veterans find their way to campgrounds. In Titusville I helped a homeless vet. There were 200 homeless vets living in the woods and on the streets around the area. How can this be happening?

Graceland has Lost its Grace (One of our Stops)

We have vacationed at the Graceland campground many times. It has always been a stellar event. This time was different. Heartbreak hotel had been demolished along with all the shops along Elvis Presley Boulevard. (It is a very ugly space now.)

Even the planes looked shoddy. Lisa Marie should cry! Below is a shot of the filth in front of Elvis' home.

Graceland Campground

In front of Elvis' Home

A new Las Vegas-type hotel reaches to the sky across from the campground. Elvis shops can only be found in a hidden mall. What used to be a pristine location has now lost its shine. Fences were rusted. Sidewalks were dirty. Homeless people dotted the landscape. It did not have the air of an inviting place to visit any longer. Flags bearing the King's image were torn. And the campground was virtually empty. We could understand that people stayed home because of the virus, but the campground itself was in disrepair.

Diesel on the Road

Our last stop was at the Flying J along Interstate 49 in Missouri. I was shocked to see that no one at the station wore gloves or masks. I asked the cashier if she knew there was a pandemic? She just stared at me. I told her that it was coming to her part of the world soon. I don't think she understood me!

Chapter Eight

Shock and Awe at The Great Outdoors

Florida claims us as residents these days. In many ways it is a great place to save money. There is no state income or personal property tax. In Missouri, when I paid the first taxes on our motorhome, I knew something had to change. Some people create corporations in Montana, get their license plates, and avoid the personal property tax. Have you noticed a lot of RVs with Montana plates?

Florida also offers a first-time homestead reduction in property taxes and then an additional tax reduction for people over the age of 65. Yet Florida makes up for those property exemptions by charging a hefty price for bringing a car or other vehicle into the state. Homeowner's insurance is higher and umbrella policies that cover your estate are not as large as Missouri and cost more. Our agent explained that Florida pays out a lot of claims for hurricanes and injuries.

Finding a Vacation Home

Vacationing in Florida with an RV is always problematic. People love doing it and have been camping for over one hundred years. In the 1920's Titusville, and other cities along the Indian River/Lagoon or Intra-costal water way, created camping spots where people could stay for free. They even added amenities like showers, running water, and food. Their goal was to attract people to their city. Well, it worked, and people have claimed RV spaces of their own for decades or longer. Their families even inherit them. We have run into people looking for a place to rent for their RV and they have left knowing that it will take years to find.

The Great Outdoors (TGO)

Finding a spot to land our motorhome in Florida was quite a challenge. The Great Outdoors was our best shot at going south in the winter. In order to stay, we had to purchase a property. While we don't participate in many of the recreational activities at TGO, we gain a lot by living there.

For a small amount of money per year, we have free cable. Water is free. And electricity is reasonable. Our grass is managed and mowed. The ant and mosquito population are managed by outside sources. The community is gated. While this does not guarantee 100% security, it does ease your mind when you are away from your home for an extended period.

Other people use the pools. Some dine at the restaurants. Others join the travel clubs. Tom plays in the TGO band and others learn how to play the Ukulele. We play at the golf course. Crafts and woodworking are very popular. There is a dog play area and run that now houses a dog-wash. They have a church that many people attend. Special events, such as those on cruises, are offered regularly. There is a free movie night. One of the nice things that I like about TGO is that do not allow wood-burning fires. There is no smoke! And the list goes on!

Architecture at TGO

We have traveled the world and never seen homes like we have found at TGO. They built the resort a street or a "condo" at a time and it seems that every street is different. The newest edition, "Hidden Lakes" has custom homes. We don't believe there was a lot of custom work done before the upscale resort home area was created.

The more we circled TGO, the more we were in awe of the architecture. It was so ugly to us. (Recently I took a real estate friend around at TGO and she was shocked also.) Often all you could see of a home were the openings for the RV and cars/toys.

Where did people live? We have explored some of these homes and they are very dark inside. Some of the other homes are trailers with huge ports in front. Others are two-bedroom bungalows. All of this was very odd to us. And prices ranged from $69,000 to more than a million. So, this blog is really designed to give you a small peak at how people live at TGO.

Driveways

Every home at TGO has a driveway. Most have water, electrical, and sewer installed for an RV. We thought we wanted a driveway but soon learned it was not enough space for us.

Look at the foliage around this piece of cement. On hot days there would be no breeze. Also, when you are backed up to an area like this you are more likely to encounter wild strangers in your yard. We met people who loved being in and under the jungle. It made it cozy for them.

Executive Suites (huts)

Our street is full of executive suites. Some have been completely updated and others have not been touched in 20 years. There is a great variety. Some huts have full or partial kitchens, a bath, and a laundry room. Others have glassed or screened in porches and overhangs for their golf cart.

At TGO if you want to change the color of your front door, you have to get permission from the Architectural Committee. They love to have power over the homeowners. Some homeowners follow ARC committee rules and others ignore them.

Park Homes

I think most people would call these homes old-fashioned double-wide trailers. Some have space for RVs, and some don't.

Ports

Ports seem to be a better property to own than a driveway. We have heard that many of them are not very secure. The port can be standing alone or cover a small suite (hut). You can see a small building in back. I think they would be useful if you were going to store your RV in this spot all year.

Resort Homes

These beauties can range from simple to ostentatious. Below is a modest resort home. More room is allocated for toys than sleeping quarters with usually only two bedrooms.

The second picture is of a home on the golf course. Most of these homes look like warehouses or bed and breakfasts from the back.

The Hurricane Resort Home!

On good days I walk about five miles and choose to circle areas where there are larger homes. On a few occasions I brought my phone and cataloged the building process of new hurricane resistant homes. Most of the homes took about six months to build.

The walls are built of concrete with hurricane resistant windows and hurricane window covers of all kinds. (They cost a mint!) The roofs were made of pine, which did not make sense to me. The walls might hold during a hurricane but certainly the roof would fly away. I did not see anchors on a roof. So, the following photos sort of follow the process of building one of these homes. The prices on these homes range from around $600K to a million or more.

Concrete One

Concrete Two

Finished Product

Grand Resort Homes

Below is one of my favorites. This is a lovely home that only has two bedrooms. It was on the market for under a million. Two-thirds of the structure is designed for moveable toys.

We have learned only recently from some of these homeowners that there are problems with storing a RV inside a huge garage home. RV's have holding tanks for sewer water. That odor leaks into the house. They also hold water, and this can keep humidity high in a garage. Then there are the other smells associated with diesel and DEF. Not all is perfect in the grand resort world.

Coronavirus Pals

Many animal shelters are empty. People have decided that a pet might help them through the lock down. Our white girls, Hillary and Twinkers, are our best buddies. They are always there for us. They eat with us. Walk with us. Play with us. Smile at us. And they keep us company when the rest of the world cannot enter our home or RV. We are so lucky to have these creatures in our life.

Chapter Nine

Reflections on a Planet filled with Friends

Photo taken at an archaeological site in Turkey.

The rain had stopped and there were pockets of dead air that surrounded some of the construction sites along my daily 90-minute trek. As I walked past a freshly dug basement at Loch Lloyd, MO., out of the corner of my eye was a glimpse of a man wearing a long flowing shirt. Construction people are not usually dressed in silky long-sleeved shirts. Their punishing work wears them down. Jeans, a dirty tee shirt, and work boots is the normal fare.

This man stood out. He was not young or old. His shirt was tucked into his pants and draped around him. He looked like someone in a movie. Over his shirt he wore a red bandana, sporting a ball cap with swash-buckling jeans. From the way he walked, I surmised he was an aristocrat in his country of origin. He reminded me of many thin men I had seen in the Nicoleta area of Buenos Aires, Argentina. The few seconds prompted me to think about all the international people and experiences that have enriched my life.

"Let them eat pasta," might be a good title for this blog. Why? Modern day slave drivers have sent MEAT packing people (and others) back to work in spite of infections that have ranged as high as 1,000 at their plants. Most of those people have come from other countries. I sometimes wonder if we are all in a dream. Can this really be happening?

(Below is a photo of a homeless person who lives on this boat on the Indian River. I have seen boats like this in Hong Kong, Cambodia, and Vietnam but not in the USA. Is this a dream also?)

The blues come too easily as we wait for the virus to leave us. Keeping busy takes our minds off the fear we have going to the grocery store or pumping gas or talking to anyone. And it keeps us from constantly grieving for all of those who have passed on, or who are fighting for their lives in hospitals.

Roseville, Michigan

(The photo taken below of my dad and me was certainly around 1949. Notice the mailbox on the porch.)

My life began in a multi-cultural environment just outside Detroit, Michigan. People from all over the world had come to live in Michigan to work for the Big Three auto makers. Detroit was five million strong then. The neighbors on my street in Michigan, so long ago, came from Poland, Canada, Sicily, Italy, Germany, countries in Africa, and so much more. They spoke other languages and shared their delicious food with us!

It was a real culinary shock when I first moved to the Midwest. Where were all those mom-and-pop ethnic restaurants? I thought that living with multiple ethnic groups was normal, but I was wrong.

Above is a woman reading the Torah.

Saint Louis University

Graduate school brought friends from Nigeria, Japan, and Lebanon. I learned about the awful life of females in Nigeria, the crushing economy in Hokkaido, Japan, and the war in Lebanon. There were also Jewish professors who taught me to speak and read Classical and Modern Hebrew. I also learned about the rituals and beliefs of various Jewish divisions, and they brought me to the edge of understanding political issues in Israel. My main mentor was from Ireland, and I learned a lot about abuse, and white male supremacy from him.

Remembering Colleagues

With fond memories I think of international academic colleagues who befriended and supported me in my quest to bring the world to my students. There was a computer scientist from Iran, a geography professor from Nepal, a construction professor from Saudi Arabia, a very close friend from Malaysia, a library Dean and Provost from India, a Religious Studies professor from Ghana, a Sociologist from Taiwan, and so many other wonderful people. Below is a photo of the Hassan II Mosque in Casablanca, Morocco.

University of Central Missouri

During my long career as a professor, I made it a point to share faiths from other cultures (and minority faiths in our own culture) with my students and the entire university. There was the Nation of Islam, Bahai, Islam, multiple points of view from Rabbis, Jehovah's Witnesses, Latter Day Saints, Soka Gakkai and other Buddhist sects, religions from India, Sikhism, Hare Krishna, Wicca, Shinto, and New Religions from all over the world. The list is too long to share here. One Swami representing Kriya Yoga interested over a thousand people on campus.

These very diverse peoples with multiple points of view expanded my life and the lives of others on campus. Many of the representatives of the religions, I call friends. Listening to them express the love for their faith and how it could help people was inspiring. Scientology, often misunderstood, brought many people back to a normal life. And that inspiring story could be told of almost every religious leader I met.

Travel Makes Life Better!

Discovering the planet was one of my primary goals in life. I am so happy that I found a spouse who also wanted to travel. To that end, Tom and I have traveled to approximately 80 countries (probably more). Many we have visited more than once such as: Italy, China, Turkey, Australia, Japan, New Zealand, Inner Mongolia, and Tom flew to Belgium 52 times while working. People always ask, "What is your favorite country?" ***And our response is that every country is our favorite.***

The Beauty of other Cultures

It is difficult to forget the beautiful Thai faces, or the children surrounding Tom on the Bund in Shanghai. Dining near the ocean in Freetown, Sierra Leone, or visiting the Hassan II Mosque in Casablanca, Morocco are experiences that change you. Visiting Bath, Stonehenge, and touring London were stellar events. India's overwhelming poverty can be juxta positioned against the Muslim Taj Mahal, Red Fort, or Khajuraho! Egypt's pyramids, the Wailing Wall in Israel, and the Parthenon in Greece were among our first explorations.

We met informative Muslims, Christians, Jews, Buddhists, Hindus, and more along the way. (Above is a photo of a Sannyasin or holy man in India.) We learned to appreciate all sorts of architectures. Every country taught us their history. Spain treated us to both Colonial and Moorish art. At times it can be thrilling to travel.

And there are people who we will never forget. There was a First Nations Park Ranger in Canada who told a story we could not believe. A Maori tour guide challenged my students to embrace diversity as they met several islanders for the first time. In Marrakesh, Morocco a very astute older man navigated us through the marketplace.

Once you meet the people and Stave churches in Norway, you won't want to leave either. (The photo above is of St. Bas

Cathedral in Ghent, Belgium. One of my favorites.) Nord Capp was at the end of a great journey. We wanted to move to Australia or Belgium. And once when Tom had to have emergency surgery in Belgium, they took care of him and charged him virtually nothing for their help. Every people, every country, every experience has made our lives rich and full. We often wished that our faces matched the faces in the countries we visited -- because they were so beautiful.

Traveling through Eastern European countries made us weep. While we could have taken up residence in Budapest, Hungary, other countries have not recovered from the awful effects of Communism. We learned about the wholesale slaughter of Jews in Novi Sad and the killing of the Croatian peoples by the Serbs. (Above is a shot of the Hungarian Parliament Building. Glorious!)

The Tunes in our Minds

Architecture and food are basic to any trip, but as we traveled, we listened to music that penetrated our hearts. I will never forget the drumming in Japan or the chants of the monks in Nepal. Muslim Calls to Prayer in Egypt, Turkey, or Morocco were beautiful sounds that filled the air. And brothers chanting in Ireland and throughout Europe in great cathedrals was enthralling.

Puppet plays in Vietnam and Cambodia exposed us to very high-pitched music that we had never heard. And then there was dancing! Energy infused set dancing in Ireland was loud and exciting compared to the choreographed long-fingernailed dancers in Thailand. To visit a country and a people is a way to step into the historic and current lives of others. Travel is the best way to educate yourself! Below is a photo of Buddhist monks in Nepal.

DeLaval and its People

Below is a photo taken in Hohhot, Inner Mongolia of Quan-Yin, the Goddess of Compassion. DeLaval people found a translator for me. The high school teacher/translator helped me find the grasslands and historic sites of Inner Mongolia. He even found a place where I could dine without becoming ill. He was wonderful and is still my friend.

Finally, I must remember many of the people who generously gave of their time to us while Tom was employed at DeLaval. Sten was our first crusader who took us through the inside and outside of Sweden and Belgium. He was so generous. Others in Belgium treated us to home-cooked meals and tours of Bruges, Antwerp, Ghent, and more. They popped (often) for gourmet meals and desserts.

Kanda Shrine in Tokyo

A friend in Japan took us to Kamakura and paid for our fare on the Shinkansen to Kyoto. He even booked our hotel for us. When I returned to Japan, this same friend and his wife, took me to Senso-ji Temple complex. And we learned so much about WWII at the Yasukuni Shrine in Tokyo from them.

When we visited Argentina and Uruguay, several DeLaval people hosted us, fed us, and toured us around the countries before we headed to Machu Picchu in Peru. (Above is a photo of "La Mano del Punta Este," in Uruguay.)

On the way to Machu Picchu, while visiting Cuzco, I sat in the courtyard in front of the Cathedral de Santa Domingo and felt as I had lived there in the past. What a feeling it was! I loved Cuzco.

Machu Picchu

I will be forever grateful to DeLaval itself and the people who worked with Tom. They were so gracious and opened their hearts and lives to us. We will never forget!

The thoughts in this blog are miniscule when compared to ALL of the international people and places that have become part of our lives. How do you say, "THANK YOU!" to the world and to its peoples? We have been so fortunate! (Below is a photo of the Sacre' Coeur in Paris.) It is a long walk from the city center and up the hill, but it is worth it!

Chapter Ten

Underwater Archaeology

When you think of Florida, what comes to mind? There is sand. There are beaches, rivers, lakes, the ocean, and the Gulf of Mexico. There are warm comforting breezes, palm trees, and lots of explorations and adventures. Who thinks about the past when the present is so inviting?

While training to be a docent at the Brevard Museum of History and Natural Science last year, I spent a lot of time with people who lectured on the Windover Archaeological Exhibit at the museum. (Picture above is in the exhibit.) Questions kept popping up in my mind that no one could answer. Many of the people suggested that Windover was an archaeological first in several categories. My ears perked up!

The image above is an artist's conception of one of the 168 (skeletons) graves found at Windover. (The head is on the right side and body is covered with woven material.) For over 1,000 years, roughly 6-8,000 years ago, inhabitants buried their peoples here. The deceased were buried in a shallow pond, covered with woven palm fiber, and then held down in the pond with sticks.

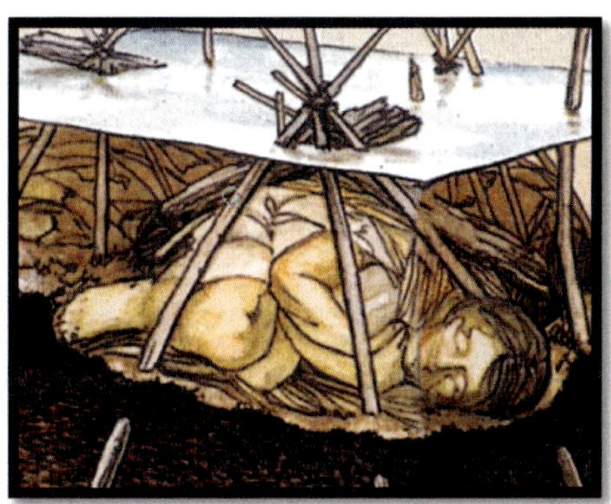

I had a lot of questions. Were there other pond sites? How old were those sites? Why were the bones preserved but the skin was missing in 168 skeletons? Did other sites preserve palm fibers or gourds? Were people sacrificed and then buried here? Can we detect violence on any of the skeletons? Why did people use this same site to bury the dead for a thousand years? How does this site compare with bog sites around the world? Did they find evidence of occupation around the graves?

During my master's and Ph.D. classes I studied archaeology and planned to be an Egyptian archaeologist. I still have my Egyptian Hieroglyphics grammar! But my favorite archaeologist died in the field because he was too far away from a hospital. That changed my mind, but it did not change my love of archaeology.

While working at a small college, I taught a class in archaeology and even took my students on a dig to a local farm. The students below are doing surface exploration in order to find a good spot to dig.

And Tom and I have experience working in and viewing archaeological sites. We spent several days in Michigan volunteering at the Ft. Michilimackinac dig one summer. We have also visited archaeological sites from the Terracotta army in Xian,

China to Tuzigoot in Arizona, and around the planet. I was funded by a university to work in Caesarea, Israel, but the dig was not funded, so the university allowed us to visit sites in Egypt, Israel, and Greece.

When I heard people discuss the dig at Windover, I knew I had to find out the facts for myself. This led me to study as many water/pond sites that I could in Florida. I discovered eleven other pond sites in Florida. We will explore them soon.

Let's talk about Archaeology before we proceed. What is it? How do they do it?

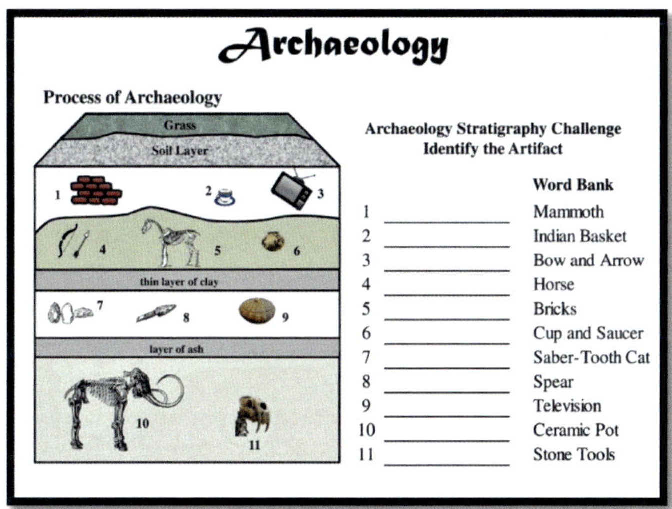

Above is a little exercise. (This image was on the web without any identifiers.) Archaeologists want to discover the past. They find objects through surface exploration, or they might use resources such as LiDAR or Google Earth to locate a specific site. When they find the site, they map off grids or squares and carefully remove one layer of earth/soil at a time. You can see the top layer/strata in this drawing is full of recent items. The bottom later is the oldest and that is where they find the Mammoths. Sites are often dated through examining pottery styles, arrow heads, wooden artifacts, pollen, soil, and more.

Underwater Archaeology

Permission to use the next three photos was given by Bureau of Archaeological Services, Florida Division of Historical Resources.

Underwater archaeology investigates sites, such as: shipwrecks, harbors, ponds, and flooded land sites. Because I taught classes about Middle Eastern Religions, I was familiar with some of the work of the underwater explorer and inventor, Jacques Cousteau. But I had never studied underwater archaeology in the United States. Above is an archaeologist laying grid lines to explore the bottom of the river/ocean. Below an archaeologist using a side scan and the photo immediately blow is of an archaeologist taking notes.

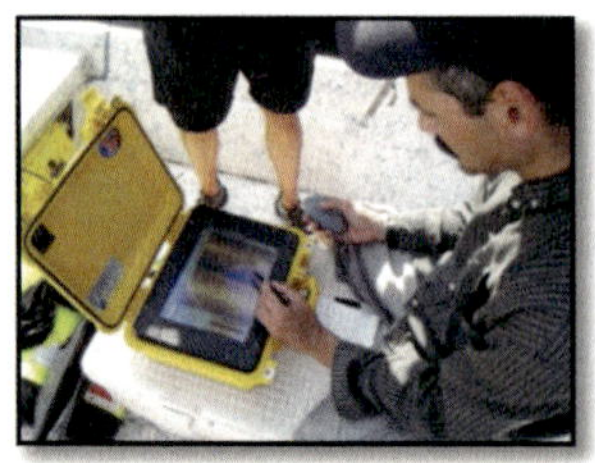

This is a photo of treasures found near Sebastian Inlet State Park at the McLarty Treasure Museum. There is also a gold museum in Sebastian, Florida, Mel Fisher's Treasure Museum.

During the 1970's and 1980's self-contained under water breathing devices became more popular and affordable (Aqua-Lung was the first.) This led to a slew of divers to begin looking for treasures beneath the seas. Eventually Scuba diving emerged! Most academics/professors ignored early finds in rivers, ponds, and springs. They viewed Scuba diving as a sport that had nothing to do with discovering the past. (Photo below courtesy of the Florida Division of Historical Resources.)

One of the earliest amateur archaeologists in Florida was William R. Royal (pictured above). Around 1959 while diving at Warm Mineral Springs and Little Salt Spring, he discovered skeletons. Today we know that those skeletons date back to at least 10,000 years ago. At the time that Royal was making these discoveries, academics thought that people had only been in Florida for about 3500 years. By the 1970's academics realized the importance of what Royal had found and began to support him and others in their search.

Look at the Little Salt Spring sketch below. On the top of the drawing are buildings. The spring used to be about where the dark green is located. (Many thanks to Steve Daniels for permission to use the drawing below.)

Hundreds of years ago, it was shallower. It is now 245 feet deep. Fresh water is on the top of the spring, but it is oxygen-depleted below. This water preserved the remains of people and animals. Can you see a ledge? or more? One ledge was at 52 feet and another at 89 feet. The human remains were found on the ledges, even a giant cooked tortoise.

Why is the spring so deep?

Before the great glacier melt, Florida's coastline was at least 140 miles wider. As the seas rose Florida became smaller. In order to survive, people moved to places where fresh water was appearing. Little Salt Spring was one of those places. Below is a slide that gives an outline of the coasts from two perspectives. (ya=years ago)

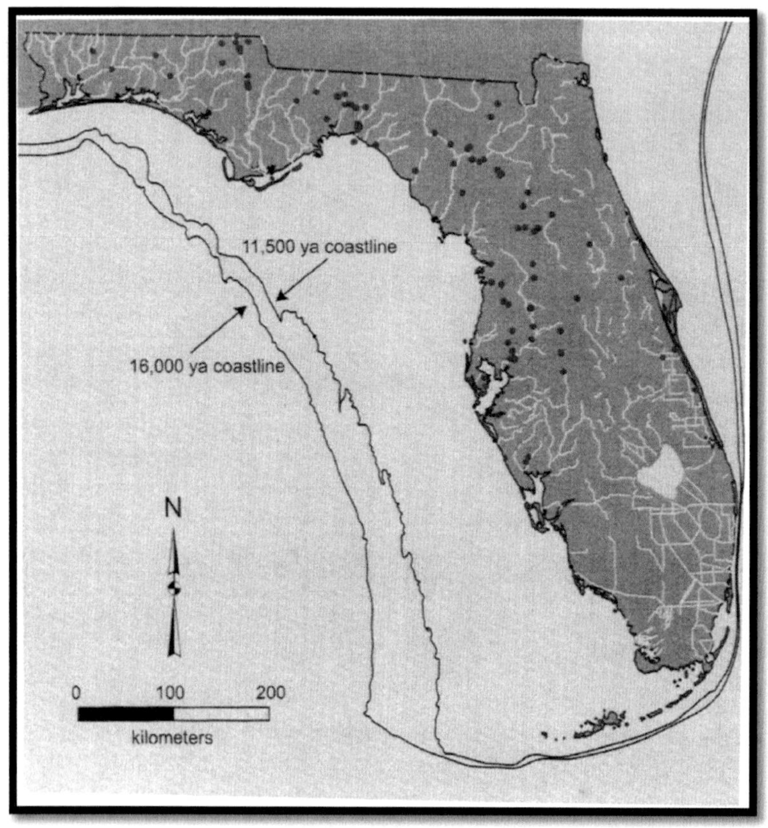

I am not a geologist, but I have read that fresh-water springs began to emerge, especially in the north of Florida as the coastline diminished. Peoples began to build their lives around these springs and rivers.

Many of our minds are filled with images of half-naked ancient peoples in Florida roaming around looking for food. (As an aside, have you noticed that museum specialists almost always portray indigenous folks as half-naked, even in cold climates.) Reality is much different. Many modern-day archaeologists hold disdain for the term "hunter-gatherers." They say it diminishes our respect for peoples of the past and negates discussion about villages and living spaces built by these peoples thousands of years ago. Those ancient humans were not like wild animals constantly looking for food to survive.

Investigating Ponds

For some reason the peoples in various times in Florida, buried their deceased in ponds. No one knows exactly why they did this? Some argue that it had to do with religion. Most of the people I talked with about Windover did not know about all the mortuary pond sites in Florida. I began to read and became overwhelmed by the amount of work that had been done discovering these sites. To help me keep the sites straight, I created a spreadsheet. The research is too large to include in this book.

The more that I studied these sites and the peoples from so long ago, the more I realized how sophisticated they were. There is evidence of trade that follows the Gulf of Mexico to Cuba and Florida and beyond. For instance, if you find pottery that uses a special soil not found in the place the pottery is discovered, then you know that there was trade. You know that people were moving around. Fourteen thousand years ago, Florida was much closer to Cuba.

Answering My Questions

The ancient inhabitants of Florida were very much like us. They enjoyed being near the water, feeling ocean breezes, and in certain centuries, the warm climate. Discovering their lives is like discovering our own past. In cultures that do not have a written language that we can recognize, we must dig to find the answers.

1. Did the Floridians at Windover cross the Bering Strait/Land bridge?

After DNA analysis of brain material found in skeletons at the Windover Archaeological Dig, scientists could not verify that the people at Windover had the same DNA as most ancient Americans. Some White Supremacists groups have argued that the DNA is the same that is found in Europe. They assert that this proves that light-skinned people colonized the East coast of the United States thousands of years ago.

But other scientists argue that the match is not definitive. (It is difficult for people to abandon the Bering Strait theory.) Archaeologists at Windover have stored the brain matter and will analyze it again when better tools are developed. The Florida State University Paleo Aucilla Prehistory project also argues that the ancient peoples in Florida did not come from the vicinity of Alaska.

As an aside, long ago when visiting Mayan sites in Belize our guide was vehement about his people not crossing the Bering Strait. He kept saying, "Look at me, I am very short with slim limbs and body. My skin is reddish brown. Have you ever seen someone from China with reddish brown skin and black hair?"

This also brings up the persistent questioning of whether or not ancient peoples could have crossed the Atlantic Ocean. Some researchers today argue that they did. What is now the United States may have been colonized by peoples from around the globe long before written records.

2. Why wasn't the flesh preserved on the skeletons at Windover?

Most bog bodies are/were found at the bottom of watery peat bogs in Europe. The skeleton is usually dissolved by the acidity of the peat water. But, because of the low temperature, acidic water, and lack of oxygen, skin may be preserved. Some of these bog bodies date back to 8,000 BCE, or 10,000 years ago. Most of them were killed or sacrificed and deposited with no clothing.

The skeletons discovered at Windover did not retain their skin because Florida is too hot! There is no tannic acid in the water to preserve the skin. The bones were preserved because at certain levels in peat, there is no oxygen. That lack of oxygen preserved the bones and other finds in the dig. One unusual find was the brain material in many of the skeletons. William Royal also found preserved brains in his dives.

At other ancient sites in the United States, skeletons were buried without their skin. It is said that men from the Choctaw tribe would come and take the skin off skeletons for families before the person was buried. Some of those burials resulted in bound bundles. They bundled up the bones and placed them in the ground or a cave.

3. Were people sacrificed at the Windover mortuary site?

Archaeologists do not think so. They have studied many of the skeletons and discovered broken bones and other diseases that killed both old and young. One skeleton had a blown-out eye-socket, others had indentions in their skulls or bones that were from blunt force. There was an embedded antler in one skeleton's bottom which probably killed him. The conclusion is that many people suffered through different types of physical violence, but they were not systematically murdered.

4. Why did people use this same site to bury the dead for a thousand years? Did they find evidence of occupation around the site?

No one really knows why people were buried in the same site. It did not make sense to me that the people who used this burial pond were hunter-gathers who traveled most of the time. A thousand years is a long time and people must have lived permanently in the area. When Windover was discovered most of the ground around it had been disrupted. I read in one journal article that there was evidence of fire pits. But the archaeologists did not explore the countryside around the cemetery. A housing development was in progress at the time.

In other parts of the world families have places where they bury their kin, where you can find grave sites or caves with multiple skeletons. Near the Mississippi River in what is now Missouri, it appears that people were buried at certain heights in the landscape. Archaeologists theorize that there was a class system that dictated where a person could be buried.

Where I grew up in Michigan, the Roman Catholics had their cemetery. The Jews had their cemetery and the wealthy had theirs. The common folks were buried in public cemeteries. And, we have found areas all over the United States where light-skinned people and dark-skinned people had separate cemeteries in very small towns. Archaeologists have not yet deciphered if there were separate family graves, etc. at Windover.

I wonder if burying in shallow water had anything to do with their religious beliefs in an afterlife? If so, then they might believe that they would be together in death?

Other Pond Sites: Key Marco

One of the oldest excavated pond sites was at Key Marco. Around 1896 a rather eccentric F. H. Cushing found thousands of artifacts. The story is long. Cushing claimed to be an archaeologist but scientific approaches to digging had not been invented. In a watery burial area, he discovered wooden artifacts which is very unusual in Florida. (Although a huge wooden statue has been found in the river near Hontoon Island State Park.)

Cushing and company dug up the artifacts but did not understand that by doing so, they were destroying them. Many ended up turning to dust. Some artifacts survived. There was no employment of stratigraphy, and today, dating of the objects is almost impossible. Below are drawings from an 1896 report.

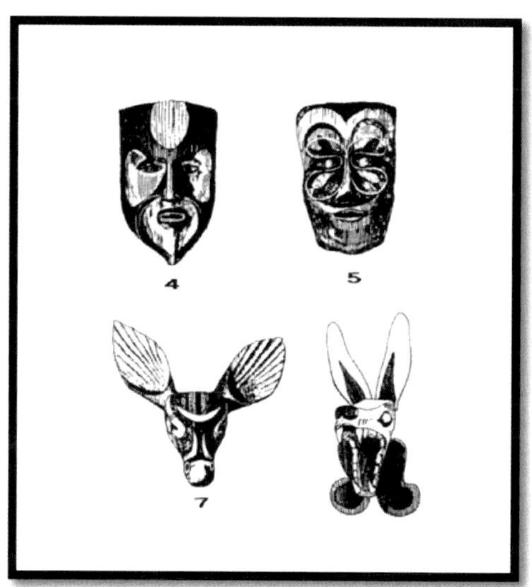

Few bones have survived, although the pond was a burial cemetery. Archaeologists suggest that the bones turned to dust also. In Kansas City, a family spent most of their savings discovering and uncovering a mid-nineteenth century steamboat, carrying supplies to settlers, that sank in the Missouri River. Today they have placed their finds in what is called, *The Arabia Steamboat Museum.* Researchers quickly discovered that boots, cloth items, and more, were turning to dust and needed to be placed in a preservative. Photo taken from Wikipedia Commons.

Fort Center

Look at this rendering of Fort Center below. There is a mortuary pond and above it is a staging area for the deceased. Notice that on top of the mound is a building and there is a meeting room to the right. There are carvings of birds around the central platform over the water.

Fort Center was occupied for at least 2,000 years dating back to 450 BCE. (So, it is not as old as the Windover site.) Archaeologists found bird carvings and post holes indicating that there had been buildings in this place. Within the area they found 150 bundled skeletons (bones in a bag with flexed arms/legs). They were buried in 4-5 feet of water similar to Windover. A LiDAR sweep of the area discovered 4 circular ditches with an outer circle of 1197 feet

Manasota Key in the Gulf of Mexico

Manasota key a new site that has not been totally excavated. This find really opens up possibilities of discovering how peoples lived and died before the ice melt. Many villages may be on the bottom of the Gulf of Mexico. In 2016 an amateur diver found human bones in 21 feet of water about 900 feet from shore. Archaeologists have since discovered jaw bones, teeth, and wood. They argue that it is a gravesite similar to Windover. I have been told that archaeologists are prevented from digging in cemeteries in Florida right now because of a new Florida statute protecting skeletons.

From Access Genealogy. A Free Site

Employment of Modern Technology

How do archaeologists find the underwater sites? Archaeologists employ:

<u>LiDAR</u>: is a laser technology that uses light to measure and uncover artifacts.

<u>Magnetometry</u>: This technology helps archaeologists to peer into the ground and identify what lies beneath without having to dig.

<u>Side-scan Sonar</u>: Sound waves are bounced off the seabed and used to create an image of large areas of the sea floor.

They also use down-to-earth methods of methodically piloting a boat in lines over a section of water using GPS which is then transferred to a map of the area. According to one article, there are over 200,000 historical and archaeological sites in Florida. Amazing! I better start researching. If you are interested in underwater archaeology a good place to begin is, Roger C. Smith, Editor, *Submerged History. Underwater Archaeology in Florida*, Pineapple Press, 2018.

Chapter Eleven

Georgia on our Minds

The highways to Florida are rife with bumps, cranks, cracks, and jumps. While RVing across the United States we often need a break from being thrown into the air by unkept highways that have been abandoned by local governments. Georgia offered us some interesting sites to investigate and rest our aching muscles.

I spent almost every summer of my childhood visiting Aunt Thelma in Rossville, Georgia. We would visit mama's folks in Pine Knot and Williamsburg, Kentucky and then head south to visit my father's relatives in Soddy-Daisy, Tennessee and Georgia.

Etowah Mounds

We have vacationed in Georgia many times but never knew there were so many interesting historical sites. Why didn't we know? Georgia has a helpful flyer with a map that pinpoints interesting historical sites in the state.

Etowah Indian mounds was our first stop. (They were six stories high--that is sixty feet!) While studying underwater archaeology, I discovered that there were shell mounds all over Florida and the world. Then, after visiting Cahokia Mounds right outside St. Louis, I found that mounds are also found throughout the United States.

Fascinating aspects of this archaeological site were that there was a moat/canal dug all around the whole village. And right above the moat the indigenous people built a wooden fence. Etowah was built on a river and the people dug canals so that the water would move around the complex. There was one area that had obviously been dug as a holding area for water. Perhaps they kept fish in it?

The moat and small lakes are still visible today along with the canal they dug to divert water. What an engineering feat of people who lived over 2,000 years ago! (The mounds were constructed around 1000 CE.) This canal/moat would provide close access to water, but more than that, it could flush away human waste.

Poverty Point is at the top of my list to visit. Some of the finds were similar. Two sculptures were also found in a pit below one of the mounds at Etowah. They remind of sculptures found in ancient Sumer over 5,000 years ago.

This site was abandoned around 1550 CE, about the time of the Spanish invasion. Who knows if the Spaniards killed and looted the site, or the people died of smallpox/other diseases? Several burials were found beneath a mound.

Like almost every other archaeological site, people had looted the mounds before the archaeologists arrived. It was a rewarding day to walk around the site, think about the people who lived here so long ago, and explore the moat/canal/river and mounds. The museum tells its story quite well. Visit it someday, if you can!

New Echota. The Cherokee Capital In 1825

The Tavern

Tom and I have visited Sequoyah's cabin in Oklahoma. It is odd that the tourist site never mentioned that he lived in Tennessee, (near my father's home), and then moved to New Echota. Perhaps we did not read enough of the material to discover his home in Tennessee.

Sequoyah created an alphabet for the Cherokees. In New Echota they printed a newspaper in both English and Cherokee. There is also a tourist center featuring Sequoyah along I75 in Tennessee. The Eastern Band of the Cherokees claim it is his birthplace. The Cherokees dominated land throughout the South and Eastern Atlantic coast. Eventually they lost it while battling the Europeans who thought they deserved their land. Remember that mythological belief in "Manifest Destiny?"

Sequoyah

Printing House

Having lost parcels of their land, Cherokees decided to create a capital that was approved by the U.S. Supreme Court. This meant that they could govern themselves apart from the United States. They were their own state, so to speak! People began to build homes in New Echota. The well-organized town even had its own courthouse and tavern.

I was very interested in New Echota because my grandmother Selvidge was Cherokee. While I have not lived in a Cherokee community, both my mother's family and my dad's family lived on and near Cherokee land. When I researched the customs and the way Cherokees lived, it was the same as my parents. Selvidges are listed in the book of Cherokees in Oklahoma and were makers of long-rifles.

Courthouse

Inside Courthouse

This was my favorite home. It was the only one that was not torn down by greedy Georgia neighbors. Hand-built by Samuel Worcester, a congregational minister in New Echota who followed the Cherokees to Oklahoma. The style is very much like my grandfather's home in Kentucky that was burned to the ground.

Worcester loved the Cherokees. He helped in the printing office and translated for them. He was even arrested for living with them.

Light-skinned people did not like the success they witnessed in this little town. Rumors were that gold was found near New Echota. The Cherokees took the case of ownership to the U.S. Supreme Court and won but Georgia decided it was time for them to leave. Georgia declared all contracts with the Cherokees to be null and void. Light-skinned people overran their lands.

The President of the United States and the military drove the people off of their land. Here is a quote from *History.com*: "President Martin Van Buren sent General Winfield Scott and 7,000 soldiers to expedite the removal process. Scott and his troops forced the Cherokee into stockades at bayonet point while whites looted their homes and belongings. Then, they marched the Indians more than 1,200 miles to Indian Territory." They forced them to walk to Oklahoma. This began what is known as the "Trail of Tears." Many Cherokees died on the way.

Three wealthy Cherokees (Notice, they are wearing clothing.) knew that the Georgia government was going to take their city and destroy it. One night they made a deal to sell New Echota to the Federal Government for $5 million dollars plus receive all of the land that is now Oklahoma. (They did not know that other indigenous peoples were living in Oklahoma.) Those men were murdered for their political maneuvering. Who received the $5 million? Most of the other Cherokees wanted to stay at New Echota, so the businessmen were probably killed by them? Who knows? Somebody knew. Very quickly, Georgia platted the land and gave it away to light-skinned people so they could find the gold? Wonder if they killed any of the Cherokees? Wonder if they found any gold?

The Beauty of Indigenous Peoples

Me-Na-Wa A Creek Warrior

We have visited hundreds of indigenous archaeological sites all over the United States. It never fails to amaze me that educated people almost always portray the indigenous as scantily clothed. It seems that they all bought their loincloths from the same tailor. I love it when I discover portraits of early indigenous peoples that do not show every part of their body. The following portraits, with several others, were on a wall at the Etowah Museum. Whoever painted them certainly loved the peoples. Gorgeous!

Tustennuggee-Creek Chief

Last thought. Can you read the Cherokee word for women on the door of the restroom?

Chapter Twelve

Follow that Dream to Florida!

Yankee Town, Crystal River, and the Gulf Coast are Waiting for YOU! Yes, there is a road named, "*Follow the Dream Parkway.*" It heads out to Bird Creek Beach on the Western shores of Florida--Gulf side. On the way to this more than remarkable place, we saw signs claiming that Elvis had walked the path. Little did we know that it was right here on this very road and in the town of Yankee that the movie "Follow that Dream" was filmed.

Crystal Archaeological State Park

We had been planning for months to visit the Crystal River shell mound. The more we studied the beauty of the area, the more we knew we had to extend our stay. During the holidays we sprint out of town. Cooking and socializing with scads of people is not the game we like to play, and this year with Covid hanging over us, we knew we had to leave.

Crystal River was home to Indigenous peoples who have vanished. They left evidence of their friends and family who had passed on and built huge mounds along a gorgeous river that was near springs. Those mounds took many years to build. Some archaeologists argue that this was a meeting area for celebrating the dead and the performance of religious rituals. No one really knows how it was used.

Besides mounds where people were buried with important (maybe personal) objects, there was a large, long presentation area--like a stage in a sports arena. Some of the areas at the site have been bulldozed by contractors who used the shells for construction. In one film about the mounds, the park ranger asked us to imagine paddling down the river in a canoe. All of a sudden, high above the water travelers would see these huge mounds with buildings on top of them. Brightly colored flags and, perhaps, music would have greeted the traveler.

In Turkey, we ran into very large circular areas called Caravanserais. Travelers could stay overnight, purchase food, and keep their animals in a holding area below the rooms or out in the plaza. I wonder if some of these archaeological sites served the same purpose. They always have a huge open area in the middle of the mounds, where virtually nothing is found in the plaza or open areas.

Unfortunately, the museum was closed due to Covid. If you google the site your will find photos of artifacts. Wish we knew who created them! Archaeologists link the culture and artifacts with several groups of cultures that go East and North as far as Cahokia Mounds near St. Louis and in Illinois.

Three Sisters Springs

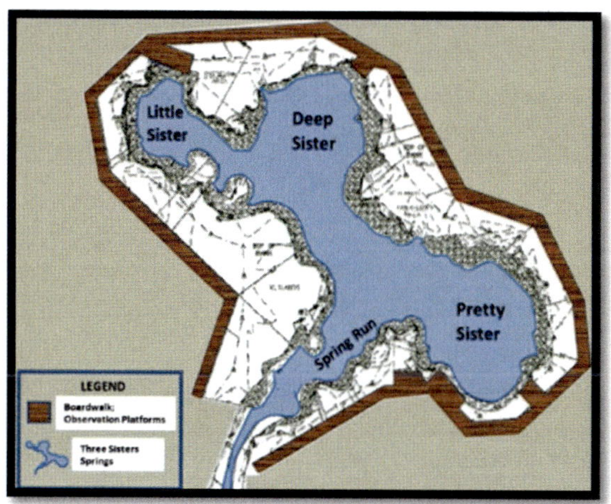

This place was a treat. It is home to hundreds of Manatees during the winter months. The water stays about 75 degrees and Manatees love it. We have a National Park pass but it only gave us a discount here. In order to visit the springs and hiking trails next to the Crystal River, we had to board a bus. No automobiles are allowed, there is no parking outside the springs, although walkers and bicycles may enter. We did not know exactly how to locate the entrance to Three Sisters, so we took the bus. Normally we would have hoofed it.

I could not capture the very blue, clear water here which is even more beautiful than the photo above. Rangers and volunteers have built a boardwalk all around the area. We walked it twice because the views were stunning.

A few manatees were sunning themselves and we followed them. One negative note here is, as the day marched on, snorkelers dominated the springs. It was almost as if we came to see them snorkel. Entrance to Three Sisters can be reached by a kayak.

Ellie Schiller Homosassa Springs Wildlife State Park

It is not exactly a zoo. The wildlife park houses (mostly) creatures indigenous to Florida. Panthers, bobcats, Red Wolves, birds of prey, shore birds, and even black bears greeted us.

Many of its inhabitants had been injured. There was one large bird who had been there for 30 years. Below are a few of the intriguing sights. The Park is well-maintained, and visitors use a boardwalk to reach the inhabitants. Some of the areas were closed due to Covid. This was the closest I had been to a Manatee--the water cow--below!

The Town: Crystal River

Tourists had invaded the town when we arrived. They were everywhere and most were not practicing social distancing or wearing masks. The main drag on Citrus Avenue sports several small shops. Some of them could only hold 3-4 people. One of the most interesting things to me was William Mickey who was painting a mural just outside the town square. "Talent" is his middle name. After offering an appreciation for his work, I mentioned that his mural was a bit idealized. He agreed and said he was going to work harder to make the mural and his love for the area more realistic. Below is an idealized manatee on the loose.

I explored Crystal River while Tom paddled around in his kayak. Here are a couple of tourist shots. I love these photos because they capture the fun side of Florida.

The Sugar Mill

While exploring Homosassa, just south of Crystal River, we discovered a Sugar Mill. On the island of St. Croix (Which we love and where we considered purchasing a condo.) we visited several mills but none of them had a huge iron engine like this one. It seemed to be much more advanced than those we found on St. Croix.

Did you know that sugar mills did not only produce sugar? They produced molasses and syrup that eventually was magically turned into "rum." So, the mills were important for therapy! It was a beautiful setting and a beautiful moment to contemplate this mill. Notice the huge iron wheel and other metal objects. In the foreground are metal vats.

Fort Island Gulf Beach

We were not sure we wanted to take the nine-mile trek from Crystal River to Fort Island. *But, oh, what a ride it was.* The road is built on top of tiny islands with water and grass on each side of you. Were we in the Everglades? No! I have a sneaking suspicion that the military did the work on this one. I searched for its history and could not find it. This is one of my favorite photos from our Crystal River adventure.

A blue haze and sky greet you when you arrive at Fort Island Beach. The sky melts into the water. Where were we on some distant watery planet? The experience was very eerie and beyond expectations. Walking the beach, we discovered a well-built fishing pier. Then, we waited for the sun to show its magnificent face. Such beauty! Discovering Florida is a bonus that we had not anticipated when we moved here. Every day we gaze out our porch and see alligators, birds we can't name, fire ants (ouch!), and huge turtles -- no snakes or black bears yet. The other night we heard cows bellowing and on an evening walk, a bobcat stared us straight in the eyes!

Hope all of you are well. It seems that the *Covid hurricane* is still upon us. Stay safe and keep busy somehow.

Chapter Thirteen

Florida. The Good, The Bad, and the Ugly

One of our favorite places to camp is Sebastian Inlet (as you have discovered). The water, beaches, sky, and birds are stunning. It is a great place for fishing, boating, kayaking, walking, biking, and people watching.

Sebastian Inlet Retooled. The Good

This year we made a couple of day trips from Sebastian. One of them was to an ancient indigenous shell mound. Wealthy people built upon this mound which was at least 40 feet above sea level. Later, an heir to the Coca Cola fortune built a fantastic mansion and grounds which were later sold. The site morphed into a two-year college and then a technological school. All failed. Finally, locals from Jensen beach persuaded the powers-that-be to save the site. They raised funds and turned it into a splendid park. The mansion is situated right on Indian river with a sand beach and more. Local museums surround it. You can hike all around it.

Jensen Beach was a surprise. A company has invested millions of dollars in developing the area. All along the river there are very cute cottages that sell for under $300,000.

Tom is checking out the local birds at Sebastian Inlet in his kayak. My favorite is the American White Pelican that can stand up to five feet tall. Oddly enough, at UCM, when I was a professor, I was given the password of "Pelican" for our mainframe. White Pelicans often are mistaken as White Swans. With a wingspan of 9 feet, they fly at least 48 miles per hour but do not dive for their food like other pelicans. In my next life I want to come back as an American White Pelican.

Today, at Sebastian Inlet, we were watching hundreds of birds swarming around Sebastian Inlet as the tide came in. Brown pelicans were following dolphins and feeding frenzies occurred around the dolphins. What a sight! The only time I have seen birds swarming like this is at the back of a cruise ship dumping garbage. (Yes, they are not supposed to do it, but they do.)

And while we were watching, hordes of other people with cameras that looked like they weighed a hundred pounds were sitting and taking photos.

Birds of a Feather. Royal Tern

Oceans are fickle. One day when the surf was very aggressive, we met a Royal Tern. She was facing the ocean. Nothing worried her. Waves would lap at her feet and the wind could have blown her away. She stood looking out at the ocean. Other birds ran away from the foaming surf. She stood strong. What was she looking for? Who was she waiting for?

Florida's Revenge in State Campgrounds. The Bad.

Campers understand that hooking up to a sewer system is a necessity when you are staying at a campground for longer than four days. Most Florida state campgrounds do not invest in sewer systems. So, at Sebastian we were hooked up to water and electricity and the water had nowhere to go but into our holding tanks. So, that means that we have to pack up everything, as if we are going to leave, and dump our tanks. (The guy below is roughing it and really prepared. Notice the drink cup.)

We have to clean the floors so the slides will not scratch the tile, and pack breakables. Then, after dumping, we return to our site to push out the slides and level the coach. Sometimes the park sites are so small that it takes 15 minutes just to back into it properly. Then, Tom has to hook up the water and electricity. All of this can take up to an hour of hard labor.

To prevent the use of water and the filling up of our grey water tank, (so we don't have to dump) sometimes we do the laundry at the bath house. (We have a washer and dryer on board.) While waiting for a load to finish, I kept getting bit. I figured it was only fleas. After all, I was standing on concrete.

In the middle of the night, I discovered that fire ants had stung me between and on top of my toes. They even bit the bottom of my feet. I did not see the ants but apparently, they enjoyed me. The sting of a fire ant leaves pustules that itch like poison ivy. In fact, these little guys made me itch from head to toe. The bite/sting lasts for weeks.

Day Trip to Flagler Beach, the Millionaire's Beach

Henry Flagler founded Standard Oil and built a railway system that connected the East Coast of Florida. His preeminent hotel "The Ponce de Leon" is now Flagler College, a gorgeous property in St. Augustine. Flagler beach is a beach for all people. There are six miles of uncrowded sand and surf, with no houses or huge condos to block your view. You can park and in 10 feet you are on a beach. No wonder it is so popular. The state RV park on Flagler beach is right on the ocean and a couple of hours from Sebastian!

How to Win the Lotto Reservation!

Our goal by tripping to Flagler was to explore a possible camping spot in Florida, and we were successful. Since we are senior Florida residents, we can camp at any Florida campground for half price. That means, that we can camp on ocean front property for as little as $14 a day, providing we can make a reservation. Recently we managed to get through the Reserve America reservation system to stay at Florida's Curry Hammack Campground between Key Largo and Key West in the Keys next November. Rules state that you can only reserve a spot 11 months ahead.

The first day we tried to make a reservation at Curry Hammack there were two campsites available. I was using my computer and Tom was using his phone. You have to get your electrode through the system by 8:00 a.m. By 8:01 you can't book a reservation. We lost the race, no reservation.

On the second day, there were four campsites open for the day we wanted to start camping. Each one of us hit the keys at 8:00. Tom chose the best site which was ocean front. I chose a site that was not fronting the Atlantic Ocean. I thought perhaps, we would win a reservation because everyone else would go for the best site. And I was right, we won.

While we won't be on the front row, we will be only a few feet away from the water. When we decide to book Flagler, it will be the same scenario. With our digital devices on super "dooper" high, we will be flexible about dates and hope we win a spot. There are two campgrounds at Flagler, one on the Indian River (Intra-costal highway) and one on the ocean. We will try for the river.

Walmart Blues. Girl what were you thinking? The Ugly.

Grocery shopping can send you to the ER. Armed with a mask and gloves, I enter chaotic space only after I find and push a heavy, rusted, basket across potholes into the Walmart arena.

Get out of the way girl!

Entering Walmart space makes you shiver. Gridlock is the name of the game. Beware of the banana snatcher and an old woman with a cane. Regularly large pallets and employees working pickup-- smash into your cart. People on motorized vehicles snip your toes without blinking an eye. Today three different men used their carts as weapons and pushed me out of the way.

Carts can hardly move through the sky-high stacks of groceries sitting everywhere. Shelves are often empty, and choices are minimal. This might account for the frenzied behavior of people who have an East coast accent!

Get out of the way girl! Girl, you are too slow!

I have not seen blood on the floor, but all the same you take your life in your hands when you enter Walmart. Sometimes whole families and their ancestors block aisles that you have to avoid. Rude and self-centered customers reach over your cart to grab goods that fall on you and into your cart. Or they open a door and hit your face while you are looking at the same frozen food. Some people are polite and say "excuse me" when they push their cart in front of the items you are trying to find. Yuk! Self-check-out is hazardous too. Machines stop working. Customers push your cart to inform you to go faster. Usually, checking out, I realize that I have forgotten items in the blocked aisles. I never go back!

Chapter Fourteen

The Taking of the Land

Did you know that Florida sided with Great Britain in the 1776 Revolutionary War? Oh no!! Did you know that Florida became a US state only in 1845? Did you know that Florida was part of the Confederacy that left the union of the United States? Oh no!!

The Culture of Florida and "The Taking"

When visiting the beaches in our many treks to Florida over 30 years, we met a lot of people who seemed to be just like us. I really thought that Florida was a Mid-western state. Duh!

After living in central Florida for a while, I kept feeling that the people around me were very much like my relatives who live in Kentucky and Tennessee. They looked like them. They dressed like them. They worshipped in the same type of churches. And they spoke like them. After studying the history of Florida, I discovered that I was correct. Many people from the Southern States moved to Florida when the land was virtually free, and they brought their culture with them.

In 1862 the Florida Homestead Act gave light-skinned people options, *after they attempted to force the original owners to leave.* Light-skinned people could choose property that was 65-160 acres and farm it for five years, then it was deeded to them. Or, after six months they could purchase the land for $1.25 an acre. Even today, when we moved to Florida, we were given a break on our real estate taxes, calling us homesteaders, although we did not buy a plantation! And they also give seniors a discount!

Florida's history is troubled.

Early in the 16th century *Spain* took Florida as its own and brought slaves to tame the jungles. About two hundred years later, the *Brits* took over the same land. They built the King's Highway that went right past the Bulow plantation. *Then Spain took it back.* And finally, in 1821 the *United States* took it as their own territory.

Of course, the history is much more complicated than this with a lot of *war and fire and brimstone*. The point to all of this is that whenever a new country took over Florida all of the lands exchanged hands. There was a taking. Whatever country was governing at the moment thought they had the right to give it or sell it to someone else. So, fortunes were gained and lost as the politics raged on. In the end all of the plantations on the East coast succumbed to what is termed the second "Seminole" war.

The Bulow Plantation

The story is long and sad. Tom and I visited the Bulow Plantation located near Ormond, Florida. I was particularly interested in the site because in the history of Florida text that I read no mention was made of plantations along the Eastern coast of Florida. We expected to discover a lovely house with gardens and people who reconstructed the past. What we found were the remains of a steam-powered sugar mill and ashes. Below is a rendition of the mansion on the plantation.

Visiting this plantation was a real eye-opener. We have visited many historic sugar mills in different countries but had never seen such a large one here at the Bulow site. It was built like a fortress with naturally compressed shells, called coquina. Below is a shot of the mill. It was huge.

John Joachim Bulow, a very young boy, inherited this plantation at the death of his father in 1823. Employing 200 slaves, his father cleared the land and then suddenly died two years later. No one knows if he or his son (Image is below) built the scores of structures that were housed on the plantation.

There were 46 slave residences and 12 other buildings including a sawmill, engine house, blacksmith's shop, and sugar mill. The main house was 42 feet by 62 feet, about 2600 square feet on one floor. Court Records and Census data reveal that John was the wealthiest man in the area. He owned 193 slaves which was more than four times greater than any of his neighbors. His plantation encompassed 5,000 acres.

Not much is known about John. We understand that he never married, was schooled in Paris, and friends had different opinions of him. Some said he treated the slaves brutally and others said that he really liked to party. In any case, he was very successful in spite of his faults.

Below is a wonderful illustration of plantations on the East coast of Florida. The map will help you identify the locations. Notice the Dummett plantations.

When the U.S.A. took over Florida as a territory, it began a forced removal of the local indigenous peoples. Or, you could say that it declared war on the Seminoles. Plantation owners had a good trading relationship with the Seminoles until then. So, when an American militia forced its way into the area, the Seminoles revolted. (We understand militias these days, don't we? And they called themselves "Patriots." Isn't the name "patriots" interesting? Image below is in the public domain.)

In 1835 the armed American guard (known as the Mosquito Roarers) chose John's plantation to become their headquarters. John fired a cannon at them to try and protect his home. He was outgunned. The U.S.A. Brigade confiscated his property and put him under arrest. His punishment was to stay in an outhouse for a year. (How could anyone do this?) Next, they built a fort and began occupying all of his buildings and consuming the resources of the plantation. Meanwhile Seminoles amassed large forces and threatened the newly built fort.

The fort was built right in front of the plantation. Wonder who lived in the house during the siege? Bet you it was the Major! In 1836 under heavy armed guard the U.S.A. militia escorted local citizens including John to St. Augustine to protect them. The Major of the militia would not allow John to take any of his belongings with him. (He must have left all of his papers, money, and treasures in that house. Can you imagine the cruelty John experienced?) I wonder if some of the Militia stole his belongings.

When the military left, the Seminoles burned down all of the plantations and other buildings but did not touch the slave homes. (I think I would have kept them and lived in them for a while.) I can just imagine all the looting and carousing that went on. And while history claims that the Seminoles destroyed the properties, it would seem reasonable to me that the slaves assisted them in the destruction. Many runaway slaves and other freed slaves joined their ranks. They were known as the Black Seminoles. To this day they do not know what happened to all of those slaves.

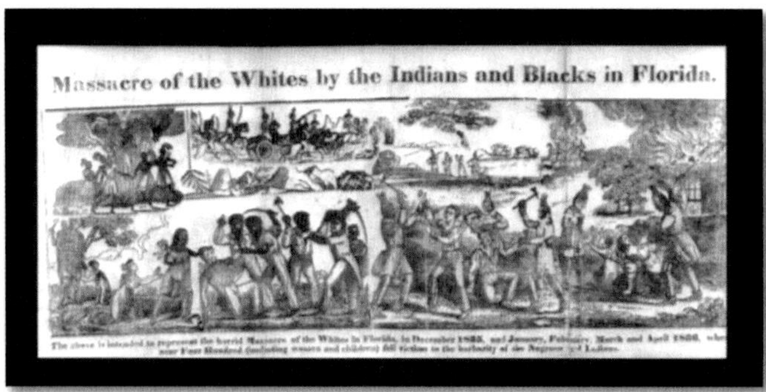

Seminole lineage is difficult to trace. Some say they were Creeks who broke away from the main tribe, or "wild ones." They resisted the Brit invasion and continually fought for their land and independence. Eventually the United States stopped the war against them and allowed them to live in peace in Florida. They won!

When John arrived in St. Augustine, he made claims against the United States because of his losses. They were ignored. He died one month later. No one knows where he was buried. His sister inherited the property but was never given a dime for all the destruction the militia did to it.

The rest of the story is too long to rehearse here. Eventually the State of Florida took over the property and created a state park to tell the Bulow story.

The 1890 Clifton Colored School on Merritt Island

Recently the Park Ranger who manages the Visitor Center on Merritt Island National Refuge just north of Canaveral, asked if I would research one room schoolhouses on the Refuge. The Park Ranger's request actually propelled me to study other communities in Eastern Florida. That is when I found the Bulow plantation. Notice on the map earlier that lists the plantations that there are two that belong to the Dummetts. The younger Dummett went on to create a famous orange plantation on Merritt Island.

NASA purchased around 80,000 acres of northern Merritt Island between 1962-1964, and even more acreage earlier. The US government came in and offered people a stipend for their land and demolished almost all the structures. Although some residents claim they were never paid for their property, and others say they were underpaid. (Here we have "the taking" again!)

Merritt Island, before 1962, was a thriving community with farms, beach homes, churches, restaurants, schools, and a great hunting, boating, and fishing tourist industry. Now it is all gone. But instead, we have the extraordinary National Merritt Island Refuge and Canaveral National Seashore.

A few years ago, remains of a one room schoolhouse were discovered with a trunk inside of it. That school was known as Clifton Colored School (see above), built around 1890. People were surprised that it had survived the wrecking ball. Today there is a growing interest in the stories and lives of the people who once called northern Merritt Island home.

My assignment was to discover how the Clifton school was constructed on the inside and what type of latches were used. In addition, I was to locate other one room schools in the area. It was a daunting task because museums and most libraries were closed. But I did uncover a few one room schools on the Refuge and in Brevard County.

Above is a look at a few of the pics I discovered. (All photos are in the public domain.) The first one was a beach house on Merritt Island. While this place is humble, the local museum in Titusville has a large arial photo on the wall of the expensive homes on the shores. It was a sad thought to think of all of those beautiful places being torn down.

People also built homes out of Palmetto thatch. Interestingly enough, these homes are very similar to the grass huts in Sierra Leon, West Africa. I stayed in several of them in the 1970's. The Seminoles also built homes out of the thatch.

Many people who lived through the wars fled to Merritt Island. The government offered incentives for men who had served in the battalions to purchase land. Children of all ethnic backgrounds studied together during the late eighteenth and early nineteenth centuries in one room schools and in people's homes.

Chapter Fifteen

Ormond Beach and the Mystery Mound

Tom and I have been exploring plantation ruins along the Eastern Coast of Florida. Recently we stopped by the Dummett Sugar plantation off Old Dixie Highway on our way to a mound in Ormond Beach. Whoever created the sign spelled Dummett incorrectly. The second photo is of the ruins. Not much is left, because people have vandalized it over the years.

Below is the Mystery Mound! Or, Mound One

I had read about a mound that was discovered in 1982 (thereabouts) next to the Halifax River. We found the very small indigenous burial mound where it is reported that over 100 people were buried. You and I could have built this in a day.

I thought that it had to have been diminished in size based upon our visit to Cahokia, Etowah, and Crystal River mounds. Something didn't seem "right" about the mound! I kept reading about it and all the sites said virtually the same thing about it. Was it a fake or a joke?

Finally, I found a report about a 1934 excavation of the Ormond Burial Mound that was published in the 1950's. (*They ran out of Federal recovery funds in the 1930's and did not publish the findings of the mound that was excavated. Of course!*)

The report was informative but left out important data about the skeletons and how the people died. The more I read, the more I thought that the mound we visited was a fraud. In the report the archaeologists said that the mound was "obliterated" and used for fill dirt, so a house could be built upon it. Huh? And the mound seemed so much larger in the archaeological report than the one next to the river that we had visited. The report also suggested that the mound was on the Eastern not the Western side of the river and about 1.3 miles south of the bridge. The small mound was only 1000 feet or less from the bridge. I guess the bridge could have moved.

I contacted the Ormond Beach Historical Society. Gratefully, they clued me in on the mystery. There were at least two mounds named "Ormond." The 1934 report was not about the small mound next to the river. In addition, they sent loads of information that helped me to put both mounds into perspective.

There is even a timely video (*A Tale of two Mounds*) where other tourists explore the mounds in much the same way we did, and they discovered the same information. How interesting! The older guy at the end of the video walks 1.3 miles from the bridge and concludes that the original mound was in that vicinity. But, notice, the houses are newer. They were not built in 1934. So, the mystery continues

Small Mystery Mound-West of Halifax River

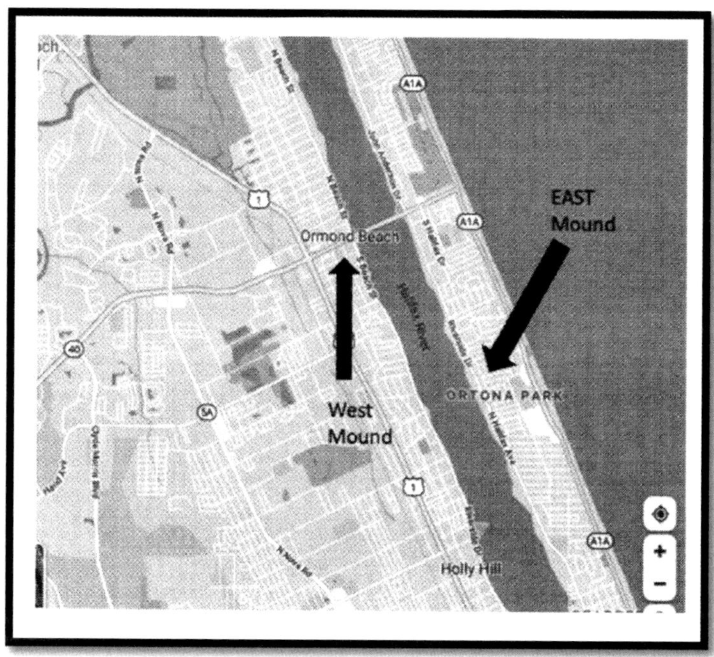

I created the above image for you so you could see where the mounds are/were located. In my view the mound is still a mystery. Researchers don't know who was buried there. The

burials could have begun about 1200 years ago and ended around the 16th century. Only a small area of the mound was excavated with bones seemingly placed in a semi-circle and perhaps bundled together.

What is most interesting about this site is that a community effort saved it from becoming a foundation for a home. Two young boys found bits of bones and pottery in the trenches being dug in the street for utilities. After several months, the city bought the property and volunteers began to excavate the site. As I understand it, they could not find a trained archaeologist who had time to lead the dig full-time. A short report was filed about the site. I wonder if the mound was originally much longer and wider. We will never know because the sand is gone.

Mound Two

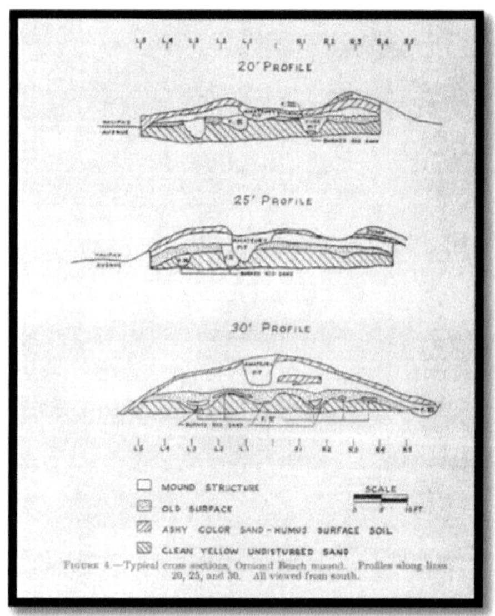

Mound Two is the missing mound. It is East of the Halifax River or on the Peninsula. This is a more interesting mound to study because archaeologists analyzed several levels/strata of sand and shells. While many pits had been dug in the mound by fortune-hunters, the burials remained below those pits. They were untouched.

If you have never read archaeological reports, the following image might seem very odd to you. They capture one slice of the mound or a stratum. Archaeologists take off one level of dirt/shell at a time. Have you ever seen drawings by archaeologists? Below is one that charts the different levels in the mound.

Mounds like this one dot the shorelines all along the Eastern coast of Florida and northward. One of the members of the Ormond Historical Society sent a presentation to me that demonstrates that there were at least ten mounds north of the Ormond mound sites. This means that there were thriving communities of people living along the shores for hundreds, if not thousands of years.

This is a slide taken from a presentation created by Dr. Jon C. Endonino on the Tomoka Mounds just north of Ormond Beach. It is amazing to discover so many mounds along the coast of Florida.

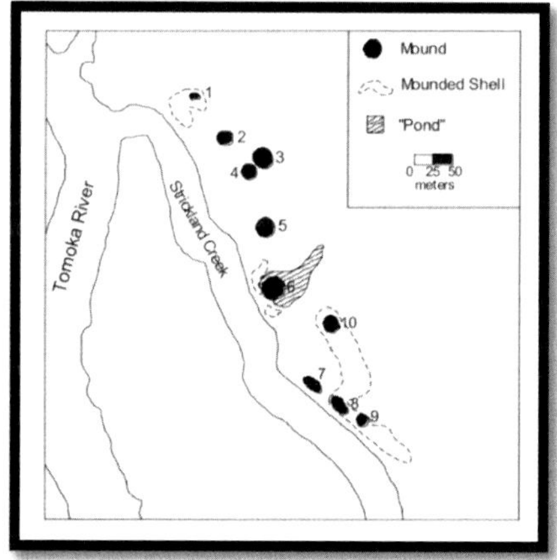

Florida locals carried away most of all the shell mounds and used them for their roads and as foundations for their homes. Some say it was good fertilizer. So, they quickly began to melt away. You wonder what happened to the skeletons in the burial mounds. Endonino has found several that still have human remains, but not all.

Below is a drawing of some of the skeletons that were found in Mound Two. Skeletons were arranged in a circle found in the same strata or level in the mound. There are photographs of the skeletons in the report that are in a circle, but I chose not to include them here.

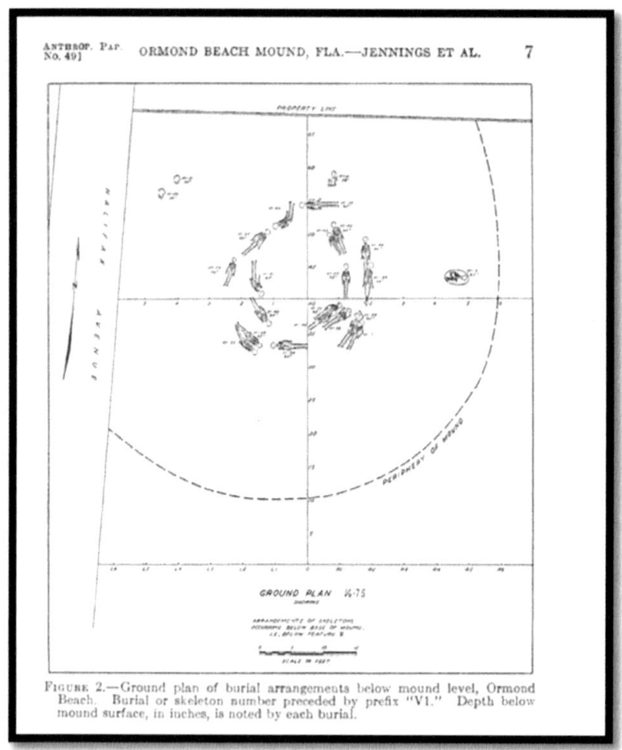

FIGURE 2.—Ground plan of burial arrangements below mound level, Ormond Beach. Burial or skeleton number preceded by prefix "V1." Depth below mound surface, in inches, is noted by each burial.

It is said that the Timucuan indigenous peoples, who lived in the Ormond area, created circular fenced villages. They also socialized and performed rituals in a circle. I thought it was a bit shocking to see skeletons arranged in circles with heads facing out and toes pointing toward the middle of the circle. (You have to look really close in the image above to see the skeletons.) Were they dancing or socializing in the next life? You begin to wonder.

What caused all of the people to die at the same time? Were they killed in a war? Was there a pandemic? Were they sacrificed? Did a hurricane kill them? Some archaeologists suggest that the bones were stored and buried long after people died. But there is no evidence of this in the report. They do not speculate about the use of a circle.

Another interesting issue in this mound were the skulls. Several were found without their bodies/skeletons. Why? Were they decapitated? Were they spoils of war? Were their skeletons stolen or lost? Did someone misplace their bones? We will never know because the answers are hidden under a home somewhere on the beach. And I am guessing that the remains are under a high-rise hotel today?

John D. Rockefeller Loved Ormond Beach

The Casements house overlooks the Halifax River. And from it you can walk to the Atlantic Ocean. When you hear the name Rockefeller, you think of money. You think of mining. You think of gas. You think of the Standard Oil Company. You think of charitable giving. We came across some of his businesses in Montana a few years ago. And while he amassed wealth beyond our imagination, he chose to spend his winters at Ormond Beach at an unassuming home called the Casements.

Right across the river from the Casements is the Eastern mystery mound and a gorgeous boardwalk that takes you under the Granada/Rockefeller Memorial Bridge and out into the Halifax River.

Many thanks to the Ormond Beach Historical Society. They responded to me quickly with great help!

Images were scanned and used from Jessie D. Jennings, et. al, "The Ormond Beach Mound, East Central Florida," *Anthropological Papers*, No. 49, Smithsonian Institution, Bureau of American Ethnology Bulletin, 164, 1955.

Chapter Sixteen

Bring your Lawn Chair!

Lake Okeechobee is Waiting for You!

Commercials with guys hawking Okeechobee RV living dot online space. ***He's happy! His life is good! You should be his neighbor.***

Silver Palms RV Resort

One of our neighbors at TGO recommended visiting the upscale *Silver Palms RV Resort.* We signed on to a three-day special for people who might be interested in purchasing a lot. Silver Palms RV Resort was clean, well-kept, gorgeous, and the landscaping made you feel as if you were in an arboretum or your own special island. People were welcoming and it was a quiet. TGO is aging and we thought we might like to live in a community that was newer and younger in many ways.

But the city of Lake Okeechobee is very small. With only about 6,000 residents, it provides little entertainment, shopping, volunteer, or tourist activities. While the town is so small, it has a Walmart, the fashion store Bealls, and a super-duper Publix with quite a few restaurants. Official tourist sites claim that more than 1.3 million tourists trek through their town. Where do they stay?

Lake Okeechobee

Heading south out of the town of Okeechobee toward Lake Okeechobee you will find the answer. The main road in the town of Okeechobee ends at the lake. Some websites say that there are 120 RV or mobile home resorts in and around Lake Okeechobee. We turned right on Florida 78 and there were rows and rows of RV parks, Mobile Home parks, and RV resorts. The map would not populate all the hundreds and hundreds of resorts around the Lake. I made a list and then threw it away!

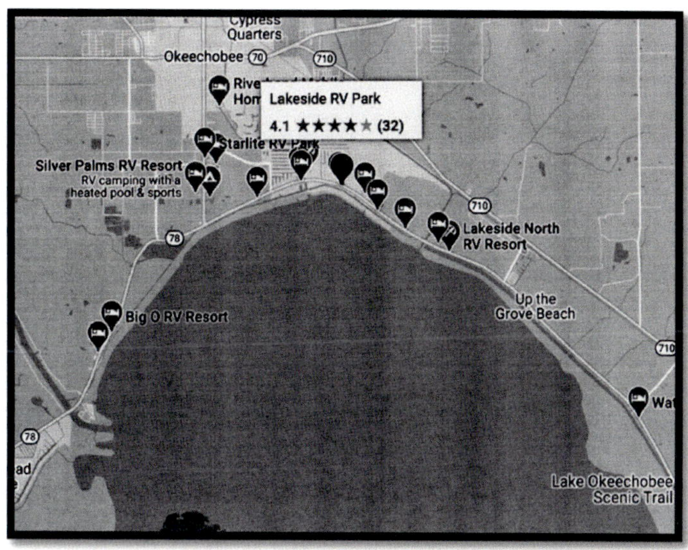

Turning left on Florida 78 (going south) heading toward the Seminole Battlefield Historic State Park we ran into a Mobile Home Depot. This was a first for us!

I was looking forward to the Okeechobee Battlefield Historic State Park because I hoped to discuss the Seminoles brutal story with a ranger. Upon arrival we found no one, no literature, no explanation of anything, and a nice sidewalk that led to locked restrooms. Florida seems to have trouble maintaining its zillion parks. Or, the folks had gone fishing!

Air Boat Rides

Tom found a site that offered air boat rides. At TGO we hear airboats almost every night in the St. John's National Wildlife Refuge. They are loud and annoying. We wonder what they are doing out in the swamp all night. But we leaped and booked passage on an airboat on Lake Okeechobee with one of the locals. They assured us that there would be social distancing. Our cruise ship at Lake Okeechobee is below.

You would never know that airboat rides embarked from the desolate site on the lake. We could not find a terminal. Finally, a guy yelled at us and said that he was the airboat captain, and two other people are coming with us. His boat was moored along a grassy portion of the lake. We had to slip down a muddy hill to take our seats on the airboat. Our guide provided us with headsets and seat belts. Throughout the ride he talked and sometimes vented to us about politics. I wondered if he was one of the people who stormed the Capital? Into the grassy jungle we went. Was this really a lake? I took this photo from the back of the airboat.

The Lake looks like/is a Swamp!

Within seconds of strapping down, the pilot headed straight through grass that was over 8 feet tall. It reminded me of the elephant grass in Sierra Leone, West Africa. Where was the water? Throughout the hours we spent on the lake we woke up many alligators and huge birds. We could not see any fish, although people were fishing in the canal. It was an exciting and unusual experience. Do this once if you get a chance.

We were booked at the Everglades National Park earlier this year. Unfortunately, our RV needed repairs and we had to cancel. One of the things we were looking forward to do was an airboat tour in the Everglades. Okeechobee stepped up and made it happen for us.

Okeechobee Lake is very shallow and less than six feet deep in most places. (Most websites say it is nine feet deep, but it is very low at the moment.) Several spots were less than a foot deep. There is a canal that runs through the middle of it with five locks that were built in 1937 after the terrible deadly hurricanes of 1926 and 1928. You can travel from the Atlantic to the Gulf of Mexico in that river/canal. Kayakers love it.

And while many people consider the lake to be a recreation wonderland, it is dangerous and polluted. Here is a recent report from April of 2021:

"According to the most recent water samples taken this week by Florida Department of Environmental Protection, the current algae on the lake contains 120 parts per billion of the toxin microsystin, (blue-gray algae), making the lake water too hazardous to touch, ingest or inhale. Our guide said it had a lot of nutrients in it! He seemed to love it.

Cycling Around the Lake!

If you like to bike, the levee or berm that circles the lake is 140 miles long. You can peddle all around the lake. One of our friends has biked on top of the levee. It was unappealing for us because of the smell, dirt, and low water in the lake. Perhaps it is better at other places where you can enter the lake!

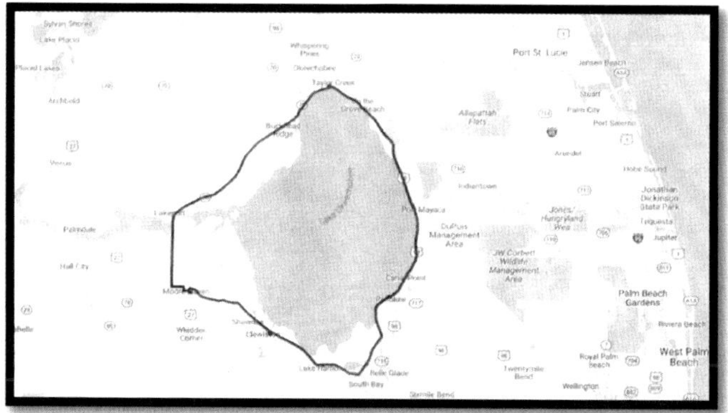

Okeechobee is situated in the middle of the state. In a little more than an hour you can reach the Atlantic (Palm Beach) or the Gulf of Mexico (Fort Meyers). It is a good place to land if you want to explore Southern Florida.

Okeechobee is waiting for you. We are happy we met her!

Chapter Seventeen

Adventures in La La Land

Have you ever heard of mountains in Florida? We were amazed at the hills as we approached Mt. Dora. Mt. Dora stands about 266 feet above sea level. The Mount Dora Golf Course was developed in the most rugged terrain! We were golfing sideways on some holes. To give you a perspective, Merritt Island is three feet above sea level and Titusville is 10 feet above sea level. Miami is 6.5 feet above sea level and Kansas City is 909 feet above sea level. If you find yourself in a hurricane in Florida, head for the hills!

I wondered how the hills developed. According to geologists a sinkhole could develop anywhere in Florida. Some areas are more prone to losing foundations than others. In simple terms the mountains are due to the erosion that produces sinkholes. As the earth opens up it pushes some land up. This, again according to geologists, occurred millions of years ago.

So, the land that is pushed up is usually sand. I noticed a lot of shells on the golf course and wondered if there were shell mounds in Mt. Dora. There is evidence of the Timucuan indigenous people, but no one seems to be interested in shell mounds.

Mount Dora reminds us of the historic towns of Westin and Arrow Rock in Missouri. It has the same 19th century feel with dreamy houses, lots of shopping, festivals galore, and great Thai food! And... it is surrounded by lakes!

Mt. Dora Beauty

Tavares is a welcoming town and the administrative Center for Lake County (Home of Mt. Dora.). We noticed that there was a Republican on duty across from the government buildings. Interesting sign! The architecture is inviting and reminiscent of ancient Greece and Rome.

Trimble. An Orange County Park

A friend recommended investigating one of 140 Orlando's city and Orange County parks. We found Trimble Park which is near Mount Dora. It had an opening for three days in the middle of Spring Break. How lucky we were! The photo was taken at the back of our camping space.

Entering Trimble Park makes you feel as if it is Halloween. Spanish moss drips off everything creating a very gloomy entrance. It is small, only 15 spots on the lake. Our space was advertised as 75 feet long, but it was barely 40. The coach is 41 feet and there was no room for our car. And our surge protector failed in its outdated electrical system.

At first, I wanted to escape Trimble. Who wants to fight your way to a lake through Spanish Moss dripping with flying things, and scary alligator eyes watching you? And I am allergic to Spanish Moss.

But as we began to explore the park, we recognized its treasures. Some of the trees were at least 15 feet or more in circumference. I wrote the park and asked about indigenous ruins and the trees. The Park supervisor (who remained nameless) answered (Post is edited.). That is me in blue below.

"This is our grand-dad tree, it boasts a 15' 11-1/2" diameter, has multiple limbs that reach 30 yards in length and is the focal point as your drive to the end of the main park road. It is a southern live oak, and many years ago its age was guessed at over 100+ years just based on the diameter of the trunk. This tree has withstood Hurricanes Charley, Frances, Jeanne

and most recently Irma in 2017 and never budged in those tremendous storms." I think the tree is 500 years old.

As we wandered about the park, I kept wondering why the city purchased the land in 1978? As we learned while visiting Mt. Dora, Lake

County just down the road has a thousand lakes. Why did a county so close need another lake? I wonder if there are indigenous ruins on the property. The supervisor would not speak to the Indian presence. There is no swimming at any of the "alligator lakes," and besides, the water is polluted.

Trimble is a great place to spend an afternoon exploring the ancient spaces. Take bug spray! (Don't camp here! Huge cockroaches fell out of the trees and invaded our RV. I think we have finally eradicated them.)

Covid Tourism

Long ago I decided that the only vaccine for me was Johnson and Johnson. (Was it a mistake?) While camping at Trimble, J&J vaccine became available the following weekend. We both tried for an appointment and finally Tom landed one near Panama City. It was the last available vaccine appointment in the state. He made the appointment. Panama City was about 360 miles away. We started figuring the costs of an 800-mile round trip just for a vaccine shot.

Yes, you guessed. We went for it. We expected to do a little touring around when we arrived and before we left. The catch was that we had to find a place to stay. Tom found one at a wharf, Gulf Oaks RV Park. (Don't Camp here! It is dangerous.) So, off we went.

I began remembering the hurricane that hit Panama City and Mexico Beach a few years back. What had we done? What kind of shape was the city going to be in after only two years after the hurricane?

Upon arriving to a dilapidated mobile home park that did not take credit cards and had no office, we became stuck in the sand. Wrecked by the 2018 hurricane, new owners were trying to rebuild the place with sand. What a mess! (I decided not to take pics of the place because it was so bad. I felt as if I was invading people's lives and did not want to feature their poverty.)

We tried for hours to dig out the wheels that had gone so deep in the sand that the bottom of the motorhome was on the ground. Several people tried to help. Finally, the manager(?) called someone (a friend) to tow us. She said that there was only one tow truck in town that could pull out a big rig. When the guy arrived, he knew the landscape and told us to park someplace else. He asked for $300.

It took the tow truck five minutes to pull us out. We finally chose a spot to stay for two nights. As Tom pulled the RV forward into the slot the wheels began to sink again. Quickly moving it back, we were able to stabilize the coach.

(The pic above doesn't look so bad, but we could not budge the RV. The wheels just spun with the back of the unit sitting on the ground. We were on a hill facing forward.)

Upon leaving, Tom had to back out because we could not turn. As he backed out, the wheels went down. What an experience! Fortunately, there was no damage to the RV. Gulf Oaks would not pay for our tow, and we did not turn it into our insurance company.

Hurricane Ruins. Beach houses are gone in Mexico City!

During our stay in Panama City, we explored Mexico Beach, Tyndall Airforce Base, and Panama City Beach. Driving from Panama City to Mexico Beach was a shocker. The land was burned and churned up. We saw the signs below everywhere. It looked like a war zone.

Hurricane Michael, at a category 5 with 160 mph, hit most of these areas in October of 2018. Mexico Beach was obliterated. They didn't even have phone service. Insurance claims exceeded $6 billion dollars. Fighter jets that were damaged at the Airforce base, cost over $6 billion. Hundreds of buildings were destroyed on the base.

Both Mexico Beach and the Airforce Base are still recovering. The sights are pitiful. I bet it will be 25 years before they come back to normal, if ever. There are plenty of drone and aerial pictures online. If you have time, search for the hurricane and its devastation.

Apparently, the owner above does not have enough cash to tear the buildings down. You wonder if he/she was killed in the storm? There are some bright spots on the beach. I think the condos below were selling for $500K.

Panama City was also hit. Signs are still dangling. Tree tops are gone. Churches are boarded up. Steeples lay on the ground. Large parcels of land are empty. We lunched at an Oak by the Bay Park where all the Oak trees are gone. It is a city gasping for air.

Panama Beach was not hit by the hurricane. On Florida 98 you could see exactly where the hurricane passed. At one point on 98 mammoth trees lined the streets again. Panama Beach is a spring break Makkah and filled with hundreds of hotels and busy people taking selfies and sunning themselves. The smell of tanning lotion filled the air as we escaped.

A Publix with a Heart

A Lynn Haven Publix was hosting the vaccine event. We were 400 hundred miles from home and my appointment was at 3:00 PM. Tom encouraged me to phone, and they graciously changed the time to 10:00 for me. I went in early, and was the first one to get the shot at 9:00 a.m. How wonderful they were to me and to us. Now we would make it home before dark! And we would not have to find another campground to stay for the night! Cost of the vaccine shot: $325 for gas. $300 for towing. Food for three days was about $100. So, a free vaccine cost us $725. Go figure!

One of our last moments in paradise this Year! We will be heading back to Missouri soon! I am calling this photo, "Seafood by the Sea." This is near the National Park site of Seminole Rest.

Please protect yourselves from this awful disease. About one hour after I received my J&J shot, I fainted in the RV. Everything was in slow motion. The RV hit a pothole at the same time that I fainted and threw me against the cabinets. I did not understand why I could not hold onto something to prevent the fall. Only later did I understand that I lost consciousness for a few seconds. The shot influenced my thyroid and crushed my back and heels. The list of injuries is long, but I have almost recovered. So, when you get your jab, don't go sailing off in an RV.

Chapter Eighteen

Farwell Florida! Hello Gaffney

Heavy hearts waived to Florida! We did not know if we wanted to stay or go! Tom had booked us in at the National Freightliner Service Center in Gaffney, South Carolina, so we headed north. The Orlando Freightliner Center damaged our RV and treated Tom poorly. We were not going back. Several neighbors told us about the stellar service at the Freightliner National Center in Gaffney, so we headed north. No time to stop on the way!

Hillary Sleeping

The pups wear seat belts and lounge around on the sofas on trips. Hillary decided to stretch her seat belt and slept on the back of my seat to Gaffney.

Wildlife in Florida did not want us to leave. Our backyard alligator hung around all morning. The resident frog kept chirping at us. And, when dined at the Indian River, a manatee called out to us. At first, I thought she was a dead fish, but no, she emerged and implored us to stay in Florida.

Converse College

In the 80's Tom found a job as VP of a Lube Company when I was teaching at Converse College in Spartanburg, South Carolina. Converse was very expensive and attracted wealthy Southern young ladies to its doors. It was a treat teaching in a Women's College. But I soon found out that I missed seeing males in the classroom.

While at Converse we purchased a home in Cowpens, SC. The setting was peaceful and gorgeous. On three acres backing up to a farm (with cattle), the house had an expansive family room that housed floor to ceiling windows. Three one-hundred-foot extension cords were needed to use our leaf blower on the driveway. Didn't they make gas blowers back then? We decided to find the old house. It was still beautiful. But the whole area had lost some of its grandeur.

The Peach

There is nothing better than breaking into a fresh peach in South Carolina, so rich, so juicy! Farmers sell their goods along the road and offer you a bite of their melon-sized fruit. Located on Peachoid Road, Gaffney built a water tower and honored the farmers with a huge peach. It glistens day and night. You can see visitors stop and worship the beautiful structure! Awestruck! We followed.

Strawberry Hill, the Stouffer's Outlet, and Hamricks

When we lived in Cowpens, weekends might find us on the road to Stouffer's Outlet in Gaffney. The store was gigantic, and we usually bought enough food for a month. Our favorite frozen entre was chili. We knew we had to find the outlet and relive the experience. But it was lost, or we were lost? The coordinates were correct. Then we noticed this tiny store with a sign with small letters, "Stouffer's." Could it be? Yes, it was, but the experience was not the same. We did purchase a few frozen items at about 50% off.

Normally we sample local ice cream wherever we travel. Strawberry Hill Retail Store called out to us and did not let us down! They sold desserts, canned jellies, and local fresh strawberries and squash. Sitting in rocking chairs out in front of the store, we knew that we would return. Take a look at the photos below!

Hamrick's is one of the best discount brand-name stores in the country. (We think!) Arriving about mid-day, there were hundreds of ***very vocal*** people shopping in the aisles. We bought a lot of stuff. Weary-eyed because the store was so huge, we left and wished that there was a Hamrick's near us.

Lands of the Cherokees

Gaffney is in Cherokee County. While I do not know if my father's family was part of the Eastern Band of Cherokees, our names are on a book of Cherokees in Oklahoma. On the way to Asheville/Hendersonville, N.C. we stopped at a Welcome Center. I was grateful to see that North Carolina acknowledged that the land we were standing on once belonged to Cherokees who had lived on it for (as they say) 10,000 years. For a split second I was very thankful to have a heritage that was so historic.

No Miracles in Asheville or Hendersonville

Tom had this idea that we should move to the mountain towns of Asheville/Hendersonville and sell our home in Missouri. We had always loved Hendersonville when we lived in South Carolina. Cool breezes kept the sweltering summer heat away in both towns. And we would be a lot closer to our hut in Florida. A real estate agent found us. Tons of research later, we were investigating homes.

We dreamed of living on a mountain top. But so did millions of others. The areas we remembered were gone. They were replaced with torn up interstates, downed trees, houses built on top of each other, and two-lane roads where locals gunned their engines and waited hours to make a turn.

Shangri-la it was not. Almost every home needed extensive renovation. Since Covid hit, people had been flocking to the area and buying up everything. Houses that were still on the market were at the bottom of the heap and the prices were hefty. Demoralized we left the dirty and grungy mountain roads for Gaffney. We felt more at home there. Funny as it may seem, our real estate agent asked if we were looking for a home in Gaffney. She could help us. No, we were not.

Freightliner Gravel Days in the County

Freightliner Factory Service (and training center) was a jewel of an experience. They serviced the chassis of our RV, by changing the oil in the engine, generator, and checking tires, replacing filters, and lubing everything. They even balanced the coach.

Newmar, our RV manufacturer in Indiana, services the house built on top of the chassis. The very odd thing about the

Freightliner site was that all the motorhomes were parked on gravel with only an electric hook-up, no water or sewer (unlike Newmar). Million-dollar Class A motorhomes were sitting on a dusty, almost forgotten parking lot in the country waiting for Class A service. Huh?

Cowpen's Iron Furnace

As usual, we investigated local tourist sites while waiting for Freightliner to service the coach. Online blogs and tourist reports told us of an iron furnace site just down the road from the National Park-Cowpens Revolutionary Battlefield. Creeping along a gravel road, we located a stream and parking lot. Even with a cement marker that said, "Iron Furnace," there was no furnace. It was a 19th century grist mill with a dam, trough, and wheel. Where was the furnace? I emailed a local historian for help but not a word has come back to me.

Treasures You Overlook

We are no longer Missouri residents, but it is our home. We had forgotten how beautiful and peaceful Loch Lloyd could be. Palm trees had caught our eyes and heart. But the minute we backed up into the driveway, the house welcomed us! (And a few neighbors!)

There's no place like home. There's no place like home. There's no place like home!

Chapter Nineteen

The Hut. Florida Style!

Renovating the Hut

My cousin and one of his grandchildren dropped by for a visit the other day. We showed them around the hut (executive suite), and he asked, "Where is the bedroom?" Well, we sleep and cook in our motorhome and the hut is extra space for music, for writing blogs, for paying bills, for TV watching, for entertaining guests, for a huge shower, and for doing laundry. I think it was difficult for them to imagine camping full-time! (Pic below is of the hut during our second winter.)

When we reflect back on the reasons we chose this property, there were many. It had one of the longest driveways at the resort so it could easily accommodate our RV. (Picture below taken from the back of my bug.) The views off the front room and porch were stunning. There were no houses behind us. The screened in porch was over 30 feet long. The hut was private with a very large shower, and it had a lot more space than anything we had seen at TGO. But...it was a mess!

Bringing the hut up to livable space was more than a challenge. The truth is that we nor our inspector could see the walls, ceiling, or flooring in the hut. Carpets covered the tile and window coverings, even with the lights turned on, made for dark rooms. Every single wall and space were filled with un-useable stuff. And this is Florida? (As you read earlier.)

Our inspector did not find a lot of problems, like a leaking roof, and so he had to return his fee. But then we were left with the issue of installing a new roof. He did find some rotted wood which the owners fixed. We also had trouble with the seller's real estate agent, who is no longer employed at TGO.

After pulling down the blue blinds that we could not clean, we found bug-encrusted windows. I had never seen dead bugs stuck to the windows and frame like that. The windows in one room took me eight hours to clean.

This year while Tom was cleaning the outside of the windows, he noticed that several were not attached to the frame. Several thousand dollars later the hut sported hurricane level windows with transoms.

Would you like to clean this?

When we tried to clean the siding, dust flew. Did anyone ever clean the siding? As we cleaned, we discovered that the siding was paper thin. Several thousands of dollars later we installed new siding.

Tom loved the shower. It was wide with a very high shower head. I would not touch anything in the shower because it was stained with dirt and full of black mold. We found someone who cleaned and caulked the space. The sliding glass doors glistened when she was done. We painted and created a happy room. Voila' a new shower!!

After ordering a new washer and dryer, we dived into cleaning the laundry/storage room. Bugs, poop, and years of neglected maintenance forced us to throw out everything in this room. Previous owners had hooked up a dishwasher (illegally) and grilled on an old table. Why would they do that? Grease covered the walls. Next to the 20-year-old washer/dryer was a filthy plastic sink. Most of the shelving was uncleanable and unpaintable. We tried to save the cabinets and some wire shelving.

From the photos enclosed in this blog, you might think to yourself that you would have saved some of the items. The problem was that greasy dirt covered everything. Someone told us that the previous owners would not pay for air-conditioning in the summer. (The cost was a hefty $34 a month?) This decision meant that mold probably covered everything at one point. It would have taken us months to rescue and clean some of the items. We could not do both -- renovate the hut and clean its contents. So, we gave almost everything to the SPCA.

An old almost-dead golf cart came with the property. It cried out for paint, love, and batteries. Some optimistic soul bought it for $1000.

During our second winter, we experienced torrential rains. Pools of water formed on one side of the house and the rain soaked everything on the porch. The winds could be very strong. Also, there was an odor coming from somewhere in the laundry room.

We soon discovered that the downspout right next to the laundry went nowhere. Water was backed up in the downspouts. We needed a drainage system and soon were digging up the property to drain the water into the pond behind the house. There is a very sad story behind this effort that deserves to be forgotten.

Vinyl windows solved the problem on the porch. They also served to keep the porch warm during cool days. I had never heard of vinyl windows, but they work very well in Florida. When I say vinyl windows, I am not discussing the frame. Instead of glass, clear vinyl is installed in aluminum frames. They are stunning, versatile, and very reasonable.

For some reason the owners had installed portable air condition units through the walls into three rooms. There was no fan or air conditioner in the bathroom? So, while we were gone one summer, we had Mitsubishi heating and cooling units installed in each room. A huge fan was installed in the bathroom. This meant that they had to cut through the walls and replaster them. We took up the slack with the painting.

Because the water heater still worked, even though it was over 20 years old, we could not ask for the owners to install one. But, when we went to install a new water heater, we discovered that units were no longer manufactured that would fit into the space we had for the heater. We solved the problem with installing a tankless water heater. The cost of the heater was minimal, it was upgrading the electricity that broke the bank.

Within a few weeks of purchasing the hut, the refrigerator broke. It had been fixed the previous year. After research we discovered that the owners paid more to fix the fridge than it cost to purchase a new one. We purchased a new one.

The hut was so small that we had to measure every inch in order to find furniture to fit. Boxes arrived daily at our door with instructions of how to assemble the items inside. As an aside, TGO is ahead of its time in recycling. They have an area where old used goods can be taken, stuff can be recycled, and there is a bin for large bags of garbage. TGO picks up our garbage at the hut every day.

This was our front room before new windows, siding, and an addition.

During our first winter at TGO, we painted about 75% of the hut. When we arrived the next fall, mildew had encompassed the outside of the hut and inside the porch. We had paid a contractor to paint the trim and gutters on the outside white. Now they were black.

We washed down every inch of our 600 square foot porch and scrubbed the outside of the hut. Tom did most of it. Then we commenced painting the inside of the porch again. This year we are not storing the vinyl windows. We hope they will stop some of the mildew from creeping into the porch. And they did.

Here are a few pictures of the hut in 2020 and the subsequent renovations in 2021. The pic below is of the back of the hut. As noted, windows were falling through the openings. Because of stringent building codes, we had to install hurricane-resistant windows. The codes expressly forbade the type and size of windows we had. So, we had to add a transom to take up the space.

Below is the front room in transition. The windows were gorgeous, but the manufacturer left gooey caulk all over them. Some of the screens had holes in them and other windows were not square and had to be replaced.

The photo below is the end of our first phase of renovation. There is new siding and sunscreen windows.

During the summer and fall of 2021, we added a room to the front of the hut. You can see the single transom (which was supposed to be two transoms), and the two windows in front. This added a much-needed office for me. All of my equipment is now out of the front/living room.

We, just like you, have tried to find furnishings for our new office and living space. Orders take months to arrive and when they arrive, we are sending them back. Everything is over-priced, and quality has gone out the window. Hopefully we can get things together by 2022. Watch for another edition of my blogs in a couple of years. Thanks for reading!

Before we end this snowbird flight, here is a peak at the Indian River that flows so near us! Come vacation in Florida and stay!

Made in the USA
Monee, IL
24 November 2021